Lifetime Income to Retire with Strength

5/4/21

Hi Neal,
Looking forward,
hearing your thoughts,

...because there is a cost
associated with living.

D1512324

Bruno Caron, FSA, MAAA

Copyright © 2020 by Bruno Caron, FSA, MAAA. All rights reserved.
Foreword by Colin Devine, CFA, CFP, CPA
Cover by Hélène L'Heureux, dga, FGDC
Editing by Amy E. Buttell

ISBN (softcover): 9781082296246
Bruno Caron, FSA, MAAA 1981-
Maplewood, NJ, USA

To Mélanie... My wife, mon amoureuse, la maman de nos deux amours, la leader de notre famille.

I love you.

Table of Contents

Foreword

*"Our approach to saving is all wrong:
We need to think about monthly income,
not net worth."*

— Robert C. Merton, 1997 Nobel Prize Laureate in Economics
2014 [1]

Americans today are enjoying longer lifetimes and more opportunities in retirement than preceding generations. The U.S. Census Bureau projects that "For the first time in U.S. history, older adults (65 years old and above) are projected to outnumber children (under 18 years old) by 2034". [2] The Life Insurance Marketing and Research Association (LIMRA) estimates there are over 50 million retirees in the United States today and by 2035 they project that number will reach 72 million. [3] By and large, Americans are meeting this evolving picture of what the next phase of life should and can be — the "new retirement" in some parlance — with hope, optimism and excitement. Hope, however, is not a strategy.

Simply put, many Americans entering retirement face a growing level of financial risk from uncertainty surrounding longevity and health costs, particularly in a post-COVID-19 world and long-term care. In addition, even a 2% inflation rate necessitates growing retirement income by more than half during the first 23 years in retirement, which is roughly the average longevity of those reaching age 65. To provide an adequate cushion given longevity trends, a plan that involves doubling retirement income over 35 years to maintain purchasing power is a realistic planning horizon for healthy individuals.

Viewed from a different perspective, the economic value and peace of mind gained through some form of protected lifetime income — once upon a time provided by a traditional pension — may be far greater than most people or their financial advisors realize. It may also help explain why a 2019 survey conducted by the Alliance for Lifetime Income revealed that only 42% of non-retired Americans believe their savings and income from other sources will last their lifetime. [4]

Out of all the financial situations facing individuals and families today, income planning is one of the most highly personal, complex and least understood. As more Americans enter retirement without the protection of a traditional defined benefit pension plan, the potential ramifications of inadequate income planning have become more apparent. When determining post-retirement income requirements there are two key variables a person faces: their longevity and their health.

But there are others to contend with such as equity market volatility, low-for-long interest rates and the impact of inflation over time on purchasing power given retirements that could easily extend for 20-30 years... or more. And while it is not possible to eliminate these risks entirely, they can be effectively managed with tools available today.

For the financial professionals who have the opportunity and responsibility of walking alongside their clients in preparing for this new retirement, the question of how to construct comprehensive retirement plans and financial portfolios to satisfy expectations and the desire for peace of mind in this next life phase has never been greater. And even more so for the vast majority of retirement-savers who do not have the security of a traditional defined benefit pension. Doing so could involve consideration of a broad mix of equity and fixed income instruments such as stocks, bonds, exchange traded funds, dividend income funds, certificates of deposit and annuities to augment Social Security and Medicare benefits.

In this book, Bruno lays out in the first four chapters some of the primary risks retirees face as it relates to creating a source of protected lifetime income to supplement their Social Security benefits. Chapters 5-11 then walk through some of the basic tools that can be used to help address these risks such as annuities, tontines and Survival Sharing. Chapters 12-16 then identifies some potential solutions that may be off assistance in creating a retirement income plan because as he so aptly put in the title to this book ...*because there is a cost associated with living.*

Colin Devine, CFA, CFP, CPA
Research Fellow Alliance for Lifetime Income

Preface

*"One need hardly be reminded that a consumer who makes
plans for the future must, in one way or another,
take account for the fact that he does not know how long
he will live."*

— Menahem Yaari, PhD
   1965 [5]

Societal Context

The simple fact that you are reading this book implies that you are alive. But what have you done with your time today, other than (wisely!) turning to this page? Unless you are an early reader, odds are you put socks on, ate a meal, transported yourself to work, exercise or a store. You spent money without thinking about it.

People spend money while they are alive! When you're working, you spend from the salary, bonuses, tips, freelance or gig income you receive from working. When you're retired, you spend from your savings and public old-age pension program, such as Social Security in the United States. On your retirement date, it is typically not possible to know how long your retirement will last — it can be a very long or a very short period.

Stated more formally, there is a variable cost associated with living. Most people don't know in advance when they will die. The fact of this unknown is critical to deciding what retirement planning strategies to implement.

Adults in the workforce typically count on income from their employment or business activity to provide for themselves and their family. Through their working years, those individuals and their employer typically put some funds aside, with the expectation that they will be used to provide for themselves and potentially their spouses, families or other beneficiaries during retirement.

Fundamentally, costs associated to manufacture a certain product can be broken down in two types: fixed and variable. Fixed costs are the costs that will be incurred by the manufacturer, regardless of the output produced. These typically include rent and management salaries. In contrast, variable costs are incurred proportionally to output production. These typically include raw materials and assembly line worker salaries.

In a similar fashion to manufacturing, retirees incur fixed and variable costs as a function of the length of their retirement. Fixed costs include funeral expenses. Variable costs typically include housing maintenance, food, clothing, transportation, traveling, routine medical expenses, phone and internet to name a few. While some of the above costs may be fixed or unknown, they will generally vary depending on how long you live.

The confluence of several factors has led retirees and pre-retirees to manage their own retirement plan in environments that continue to increase in complexity. These factors include the initial popularity of defined contribution pension plans (DC plans) — such as 401(k)'s in the United States — at the same time as employer sponsored defined benefit pension plans (DB plans) started to decline [6] and lengthening lifespans.

This has created a difficult situation for retirees and pre-retirees who must plan for a retirement of an unknown duration. It may last a few years or several decades. It would be natural to think that private pure lifetime income products would soar in reaction to DB plans fading away but they haven't. Pure lifetime income products — which I define as a financial vehicle where the individual pays an upfront sum in exchange for recurring payments for life and payments cease at death — are unpopular and unavailable in some countries.

Lifetime income is self-explanatory; it is income for life. It is created from a family of financial vehicles that turns a lump sum of money into a series of payments until death. It comes in many shapes, including income annuities, DB pensions plans, tontines and public old-age pension programs.

Yaari wrote the statement at the beginning of the chapter in 1965, a time when the average individual retirement period was approximately 13 years. The average individual retirement period at the time this book is being written is closer to 20. [7] Yaari's findings have been used for several decades.

Personal Perspective

As a financial analyst — I currently work as a credit financial analyst and previously worked as an equity financial analyst — I perform financial analysis on companies. In this capacity, I must examine and analyze a myriad of opinions, statements and regulations. At the center of these analyses are two statements: the balance sheet and the income statement.

Arguably, in a credit analysis, a little more focus is placed on the balance sheet and on the equity side, a little more emphasis is geared towards the income statement. As a testament to that, rating agencies typically develop capital models as a tool to assess a company's balance sheet. AM Best's methodology states that the balance sheet assessment is the most important step in the rating process. To deepen the analysis of a balance sheet, the rating agency has developed a capital model, known as the Best's Capital Adequacy Ratio (BCAR), as a tool to help assess the balance sheet strength of a company.

In contrast, equity analysts go through a period every quarter informally known as "earnings' season" and typically use earnings' financial models to forecast and assess operating performance. Those results are typically aggregated through the industry to form a benchmark, known as consensus; as actual earnings are disclosed by companies, deviations from consensus are analyzed and are a driver of stock prices.

Having said that, rating agencies don't ignore earnings and stock analysts don't ignore balance sheets of companies. AM Best states within its methodology that operating performance is the most important factor driving ratings after assessing the balance sheet. Similarly, equity analysts do forecast balance sheets and use that information to make stock recommendations. There is no such thing as ignoring the information that a balance sheet or income statement provides, as each tell a different story and one feeds input to the other.

For many financial professionals, this may seem like stating the obvious; however, this is precisely the mistake retirees make by focusing on their own balance sheet and ignoring the income their portfolio can generate. Retirees typically concentrate their attention on their personal balance sheet — mutual fund balance, 401(k) in the United States or Registered Retirement Savings Plans (RRSP) in Canada, total certificate of deposit (CD) values, etc.) — and the risk associated with holding those assets. However, the income those assets are able to generate is less of a focus.

In retirement planning, income is at least as important as net worth. When thinking about the performance of retirement savings, assessing it simply by account value provides limited perspective; how much income those assets will generate is the key question to answer. Given each individual's unknown lifespan, lifetime income planning is a critical tool that I believe is currently under-appreciated. My goal in writing this book is to help demystify lifetime income planning so that individuals can appreciate the role that lifetime income can play in creating a retirement plan.

Retirees' widespread aversion to income annuities and lifetime income in general is known as the annuity puzzle. I was recently asked to participate in a "bring your kids to work day". Along with colleagues, we organized a simulation of insurance contracts using fake money. I did the income annuity part, asking two children under-ten-year-old to hand me — the insurance company — their money and told them to pretend they were 70-year-old. As each year went by, I handed them a portion of their pile. Through the simulation, one participant passed away before his pile was depleted. The other depleted its pile as he was still alive. When its pile was exhausted, I shared the "dead" participant's pile as payments to the alive participant, in order to illustrate the concept of risk pooling. The "dead" 9-year-old participant yelled, "That's my money!" This reaction captures the initial lack of appeal of income annuities — individuals fear dying early in their retirements and forfeiting a large amount of future income.

This book will address this dynamic as well as the hybrid characteristics of lifetime income. Lifetime income is a family of financial vehicles that contains aspects of insurance and investments. As a result, individuals who are comfortable with insurance and investments as separate vehicles can easily become confused by products that share attributes of insurance and investments. For example, an individual can be completely at ease with traditional insurance and losing their car insurance premiums a year after driving with no accident. However, this same individual may find it quite difficult to come to terms with exchanging a lump sum of money for income payments during retirement. That's because the premise of lifetime income creates a conflict with their comfort with traditional asset classes with an account value associated to it. When confronted with discomfort, most individuals opt for the vehicle that offers the most familiarity and comfort. This book challenges pre-retirees and retirees to move beyond their temporary discomfort to embrace this combination of products, which offers powerful benefits and a strong potential for sustainable retirement planning. This philosophy is in line with the Retirement Income Journal mentality stating that "a combination of the two [investments and insurance] can create financial synergies for the client." [8]

While progress has been made at the turn of the millennium as some individuals have started to recognize the significance of longevity risk, many fail to comprehend the magnitude of this risk. As pointed out by Haid, Chan and Raham: "There is relatively little understanding of longevity risk. Many retirees do not recognize outliving assets as an issue." [9]

Financial position and income are both important in retirement planning precisely due to longevity risk. Prudent retirement planning should not overlook the importance of income and lifetime income can play a key role in this exercise.

Life expectancy has increased over multiple decades across many countries. Mortality tables quantify this statement but each individual has their own story on how they've observed that phenomenon, including myself and perhaps Paul McCartney who wrote and recorded the Beatle song "When I'm Sixty-Four". At the time he wrote and recorded the song, he most likely felt like being 64 years old was an old age. He is now more than a decade older than 64 years old and may have a different perspective of how old 64 years old is...

The increase in life expectancy contributes to the increase in longevity risk but it is only the tip of the iceberg as life expectancy is a weighted average metric that has a significant meaning for a population but less so for an individual.

This book addresses longevity and bequest risks. It also discusses lifetime income as it exists and how it may take shape in the future. Finally, it suggests a framework, the Asset to Income Method (AIM) for managing retirement planning.

This book is designed to assist readers in cogently planning for retirement and weighing portfolios of assets and expected incomes as opposed to focusing on particular products.

Product features and markets evolve on a continuous basis. The role of financial advisors and planners is to not only understand personal situations but also the context of those situations in order to explain and recommend specific products and strategies to retirees. The same applies for tax strategies. This book does not attempt to provide investment recommendations, tax opinions or other professional advice; these should be rendered by the appropriate professionals.

While most practical examples apply to the United States and the Canadian markets, this book is designed for readers everywhere. My intent is to help readers gain comfort in navigating conceptually in the investment and the insurance world during retirement.

This Book

Target Audience

This book is addressed to financial professionals who are tackling the decumulation phase of retirement within any jurisdiction. Within the subset of those professionals, those who can reap the maximum benefit from this book are those with the ability and knowledge to integrate insurance and investment solutions as part of a comprehensive retirement plan. Ambidextrous financial advisors, as defined by Pechter in The Retirement Income Journal, are the type of financial professionals most likely to benefit from reading this book. [10] Ambidextrous financial advisers are professionals who have the ability to navigate in both the insurance and in the investment world; they are able to leverage aspects of both environments in order to construct an optimal retirement portfolio. [10] The book is also targeted to financial professionals in general. It requires some familiarity with the dynamics of the main asset classes such as equities and fixed income. It also requires a basic understanding of the concept of insurance and risk pooling. Financial planners and advisors are therefore the main audience but other professionals such as accountants, actuaries, analysts, attorneys, brokers, policymakers, regulators, as well as individuals with a basic financial understanding could find interest in this book.

There is an attempt to stay away from the technical actuarial calculations, although some is used to a minimal extent and should not prevent the non-technical reader to understand the concept.

Purpose

This book offers a way to think about the use of financial resources through retirement and provide a mindset for retirees to juggle between the many unknowns they face, such as longevity and older-age health. It also puts on the forefront various strategies at the disposition of retirees from the worlds of investment and insurance.

This book is not about distribution dynamics, fiduciary issues or sales practices in various jurisdictions. It is meant to be timeless and borderless allowing readers to build a general framework and mentality that can be adapted in the various economic environments, jurisdictions and demographics dynamics. It is the role of the financial professional to adapt to those economic environments, jurisdictions and client's personal situations. The book is not a step-by-step guide to generate sales or execute immediately on a strategy in a particular jurisdiction.

Most examples are geared towards the North American markets and the economic environments at the time the book is being written but this is not a hard rule as some illustrative examples are built off different economic variables. The book is meant to be borderless and timeless; the concepts and tradeoffs are the key take away.

This book should be used for educational and informational purposes only and the reader should consult a qualified expert before taking tangible actions. Specifically, this book does not offer professional advice. Experts such as financial advisors, financial planners, estate planners, attorneys, accountants, actuaries or other professionals providing advice in this field should be consulted when executing transactions or purchases of financial instruments.

Flow

First, in section 1, Current Environment, I will highlight the current environment retirees and pre-retirees are living in and describe the challenges of longevity risk, which is the financial risk associated with people living longer than anticipated or outliving their savings. Bequest risk, the risk associated with people not achieving their bequest goals, is also addressed.

In section 2, Lifetime Income Vehicles, I will look at various lifetime income products and strategies that attempt to solve the problem. Some of these products are currently available to consumers, while others may see the day in the future, including one that I developed, which is known as Survival Sharing.

Finally, in section 3, The Solution, I will introduce the AIM, an asset and income allocation framework to use for retirement planning. It looks at both traditional wealth management as well as insurance concepts.

The appendix and acronym sections at the end of the book provide a reference to the terminology and the concepts used throughout the book.

The experts in longevity risk and retirement income planning can skip sections 1 and 2, use those sections as reference material and go straight to section 3.

1. Current Environment

I. <u>Retirement</u>

*"In retirement, clients need to maintain
a steady income stream beyond their Human Capital.
Basic expenses, discretionary expenses, legacy objectives,
and additional goals can all be met with
[guaranteed lifetime income]."*

— Michael Gordon
   2013 [11]

<u>Retirement in General</u>

In most industrialized countries, retirement planning is a growing concern for both individuals and society. As the use of DB plans has decreased significantly over the last few decades, [6] the predictability of retirement income that individuals previously enjoyed is in the process of disappearing. This confluence is occurring at the time that one of the largest generations in history, the baby boomers, are retiring. Also, most developed countries have public old-age pension programs in place but their generosity and adequacy for retirement varies greatly from one country to another. In addition, as the population is aging, the viability and sustainability of these plans can be questionable as costs keep creeping up.

Governments and employers have generally decreased their involvement in retirement planning, leaving individuals with the burden of providing and planning for their own long-term financial needs. This emerging reality creates both challenges and opportunities on an individual and societal level.

Traditional retirement planning is typically tackled in a way that creates a tradeoff between a rate of spending and a probability of running out of funds. This problem is not new: Leonardo Fibonacci more than eight centuries ago was asked by a friend, "How long will my money last given a constant withdrawal amount and earned rate?" [12] Fibonacci essentially came up with the present value of money concept used widely for finance both in academics and in financial planning practice.

The tradeoff between wealth and income has also been studied by Warshawsky. [13] It has also been analyzed by Devine and Mungan. [14] Their recent research showed that for a 65-year-old woman, the probability of running out of income during her life expectancy of 22 years, should she encounter a 20% market correction sometime within her first 10 years of retirement, is 22.3%, assuming the following:

- Investment return drop*:   20%
- Equity/Bond allocation: 70%/30%
- Withdrawal Rate: 4%
*assumed 20% investment return drop occurred randomly within 1st 10 years [14]

For a male, where life expectancy from age 65 is 19 years, the risk of running out of income under the same scenario was 12.7%. Thought of another way, while a woman aged 65 on average will live three years longer than a man, per Devine and Mungan, her risk of running out of income is nearly double. [14]

This can certainly trigger a wakeup call for many, as such an event can be catastrophic with a probability of happening higher (22.3% for a woman) than that of rolling a seven with two dice (16.7%).

Phases of Retirement

Financial retirement planning is composed of two parts: the accumulation phase and the decumulation phase, which is referred to as payout phase. The accumulation phase is the period when individuals are working and putting funds aside for a future retirement. The decumulation period begins when the individual retires and depends less on steady employment. In the past, this transition used to be clear where a worker would typically be employed at a firm for a long period of time and retire overnight with a pension from that employer. That individual did not have to be concerned about retirement income planning because their income needs were met by the pension income received monthly from their former employer. However, today, many different arrangements exist including phased out retirement or retirees working part time. At this point, the retiree begins to live on public pensions and retirement assets, accumulated through personal and/or employer contributions.

Accumulation Phase of Retirement

The period of time when individuals are working and accumulating wealth typically corresponds to the decades between when they enter the workforce (typically in their 20s) and retire (typically in their 60s). During that time, they accumulate assets with the intention of monetizing them gradually for use during retirement.

While asset management and investing are complex endeavors, there are a few guiding principles individuals understand and relate to during the accumulation phase. Generally, all else being equal:

- The sooner funds are saved and set aside, the more assets an individual can expect to have at their disposal in retirement.
- The more funds an individual sets aside while working, the more they can expect to accumulate for retirement.
- The longer an individual's time horizon is, the more they can afford to take investment risks.
- The more risks individuals take, over time the higher the expected return on investment can be.
- Diversification in various forms — asset classes, securities, time, etc. — can help reduce risk.

McSween explains this concept in the context of the era in which this book is written by observing a negative correlation between good savings habits and the quality of an Instagram account. [15] Individuals can observe and measure their progress towards saving for retirement in various ways, including the value of their various accounts. Further, several DC plans such as 401(k) in the United States or Registered Retirement Savings Plans (RRSP) in Canada offer different incentives to encourage individuals to save and can serve as a natural avenue for accumulation. These incentives may include employer contributions and/or tax incentives. The term DC plan here is used loosely as there can be nuances between jurisdictions but any asset accumulation plan, typically sponsored by an employer with tax advantages will be considered as a DC plan.

Decumulation Phase of Retirement

Upon retirement, individuals begin the decumulation phase, where working revenues are typically not the main source of income to support their lifestyle until death. The age range associated with this period is typically from the 60s onwards. The decumulation phase can pose a far different dynamic than the accumulation phase. Should a retiree prioritize asset returns, managing drawdowns, maintaining purchasing power, preserving liquidity or all the above? If so, how? These thorny questions lack a clear-cut, one-size-fits-all answer. The more a retiree spends during retirement, the more quickly they can exhaust their retirement savings. On the other hand, the less they spend, the less they might enjoy the opportunities of retirement. So, what is the optimal amount a retiree should spend per period? The question has been explored by many scholars, in particular by Milevsky and Salisbury in a very elegant and mathematical approach. [16] The question is also addressed in this book.

The decumulation phase of retirement is usually perceived as more difficult than the accumulation phase because retirees are dealing with future unknowns such as longevity, market returns, unexpected expenses — such are for health — and inflation to name a few. The dynamic is different than the accumulation mindset, especially when it comes to longevity, sequence of return and finding the right risk appetite balance. [8] I believe life span is an unknown that shouldn't be guessed. A sound financial plan should consider all outcomes. Income and bequest objectives should be targeted in a consistent manner, regardless of time of death.

Pre-retirees and retirees should consider the similarities between retirement income planning and car insurance. When purchasing car insurance, there are a variety of potential outcomes. These include no accidents, a minor accident or a major accident. To an individual, the expected damages that may be incurred as a result of driving is somewhat irrelevant because it is replaced by a manageable and predictable insurance premium.

The same holds for retirement planning; managing to a single point of life expectancy results in planning for a small window of possible outcomes, for both recurring income and bequests. Prudent retirement planning encompasses acknowledgement of a broad range of possible unknowns. It requires careful consideration of how these factors could affect savings and income.

II. Longevity Risk

*"there were clear differences in the central features
of investment for institutions
and investment for individuals"*

— Harry M. Markowitz, 1990 Nobel Prize Laureate in Economics
1991 [17]

Longevity Risk in General

In its broadest definition, longevity risk is the financial risk of living longer than anticipated. Many entities face longevity risk, such as governments offering public old-age pension program, insurance companies offering lifetime income products such as payout annuities or living benefits and corporations providing DB plans to employees. These entities usually have the knowledge, capital, expertise and resources to manage longevity risk. Further, these entities manage longevity risk based on a large population of people. There is one stakeholder who is too often not equipped to deal with this unknown and for whom the consequences of mismanaging longevity risk could prove catastrophic: the individual.

Institutions, such as insurance companies, large employers or governments have the advantage of dealing with longevity risk in a context where the law of large numbers pertains. These institutions have had success in managing mortality and survivorship risks for large groups of people. For example, insurance companies pool the risks of many individuals and accumulate assets to cover reserves in order to provide for the anticipated future outcome of a group.

Another key distinction is that institutions are typically managed on a going concern basis, which includes the capacity to adjust. For example, if scientists were to discover a cure for a major disease, an insurance company offering longevity-oriented protection products would most likely revisit its reserving assumptions based on this new discovery. Because this breakthrough would likely increase lifespans for its insureds, that company would make a provision for future expected benefits.

This dynamic does not apply to individuals; while an individual's horizon is unknown, it is finite. From the individual's perspective, the length of survivorship is an unknown. Life expectancy for a group of individuals is one of many useful metrics that provide some insights on the demographics of a population of employees covered by a DB plan or contract holders of a longevity insurance product. By comparison, life expectancy for an individual is merely the starting point of the discussion. [18] Furthermore, institutions typically have access to professional advice, as well as sophisticated financial products and solutions that are not necessarily available to retail investors.

Individuals and institutions deal with longevity risk from different angles. This dynamic is also observable within investment management where individuals and institutions may have different goals, risks, objectives and timeline. Markowitz pointed that his Nobel Prize winning modern portfolio theory was developed for institutions and that individuals should utilize different "research methodology". [17]

Planning for retirement would be less of a daunting task if retirees knew in advance how long they would live. This unknown presents a challenge that requires a comprehensive solution as it impacts many other unknown variables. [19] [20] [21]

The principals of actuarial sciences are typically applied within an organizational context but individuals can also benefit from actuarial science concepts, as Shemtob advocates through REST. [22]

Individuals typically have a good understanding of life expectancy, as the concept of weighted average is covered in basic mathematics courses. If asked how long the average 65-year-old can expect to live, most people will answer somewhere around 20 years. That leads to an expected age of death of 85-year-old, which is a good answer given reasonable assumptions. What is less clear is how well people grasp the concept of a statistical distribution, as this is generally only taught in higher-level mathematics. When one asks those same individuals the probability of dying at the exact age of 85 — the expected age of death — answers diverge greatly. Responses ranging from 40% - 60% are not uncommon. The correct answer is closer to 4%.

Club Vita published a chart (reproduced as Figure 1) illustrating this concept and points at that "Over-reliance on life expectancy figures has the danger of over simplifying the challenges of financial planning for the future." (23)

Figure 1: Probability of a 65 year old dying before, after or in the year of their life expectancy

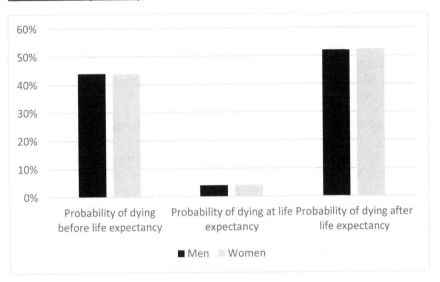

Source: Club Vita, reproduced with permission (23)

Major Organizations and Longevity Risk

Longevity risk is no longer an insignificant issue for many organizations. Many professional associations, organizations, corporations and governments now view longevity risk as a major concern in the current social, economic and demographic environment. These include but not limited to the CFA Institute , (16) (19) the American Academy of Actuaries (AAA), (24) the Congressional Research Service, the U.S. Government Accountability Office, (25) the World Economic Forum, (26) the International Monetary Fund, (27) the Insured Retirement Institute (IRI), (28) the "Comité d'experts sur l'avenir du système de retraite québécois", (29) the Society of Actuaries (SOA),

[9] the American Society of Pension Professionals and Actuaries (ASPPA), [30] the Stanford Center on Longevity [31] and the Alliance for Lifetime Income [32] to name a few.

The Alliance for Lifetime Income is a non-profit industry organization established in 2018 by 24 leading financial services firms. Its purpose is "Helping Americans address the risk of outliving their retirement income." [32] Reflecting its concerns about the importance of longevity risk, the AAA has put together the "Lifetime Income Risk Joint Committee" in order "to address the risks and related issues of inadequate guaranteed lifetime income among retirees" [33] The committee, when it was a task force, issued various papers on the risk of individuals outliving their income. The AAA also published a position statement that it "supports policy and educational initiatives that increase the availability of retirement income options in DC plans". [24] The CFA Institute for its part published the paper "Life Annuities: An Optimal Product for Retirement Income" which discusses the importance of lifetime income products. [16]

This book discusses longevity risk from the individual's perspective, including implications and related risks. While not intended to be a source of specific investment recommendations, it offers some suggested solutions, strategies and approaches to deal with these issues. The use of lifetime income vehicles such as annuities can be strategic for retirees as they provide a recurrent stream of payments from a specific point in time until death.

Longevity Risk and Bequest Risk for Individuals

Longevity Risk

Longevity risk, from the individual's perspective, is the risk of outliving savings or seeing assets fall below the necessary amount to continue their desired lifestyle for the rest of their lives. This can occur for various reasons including living too long, too little savings, too much spending, asset underperformance or inflation, to name a few. [34]

Over the last few centuries, people are living longer, which increases individuals' longevity risk. Stated differently, survivorship exposure in retirement has risen in the past few decades and may well continue to increase. I believe this is only the tip of the iceberg and that the real risk lies with the fact that both time of death and older-age heath status are unknown for an individual. This creates even more uncertainty when equity market performance and volatility, interest rate risk and inflation risk are added into the mix. All these factors, when combined, fully reveal the true cost — and the true risk — associated with retirement.

Example

How might a 65-year-old widowed father of two with $1 million in assets manage his retirement spending? He feels comfortable with this amount and wants to retire. He gives notice to his employer and a retirement party is organized. Let's look at two extreme scenarios, A and B.

Under scenario A, the retiree gets hit by a bus on the way out of his retirement party and dies. He will leave $500,000 to each of his children, assuming his former co-workers covered the tab for the retirement party.

In scenario B, the same man lives for an additional 35 years and is confined to a nursing home for the last 10 years of his life. In this case, his two children may have to help support him financially for a decade or more.

Those two scenarios, while extreme, are possible and in the case of B, increasingly realistic. Leaving a hefty inheritance is not a problem per se but if it is undesired, the retiree could have spent more while alive. On the other hand, leaving a liability such as un-paid medical bills could be a major issue. Guaranteed lifetime income as well as long-term care (LTC) insurance can help with this problem.

In retirement planning, a great deal of emphasis is placed on investment variables such as diversification, risk, liquidity, fees and service. But far less is placed on a crucial question: How long will you live? The answer to that for most is unknown, just like the chance of incurring a fire on your house next year is unknown. But in the case of the latter, that's what drives people to buy insurance on their properties. Similarly, individuals purchase life insurance when in their 20s and 30s, even though the risk of dying before age 50 is relatively small. Why then not consider longevity insurance type products in post-retirement financial planning to protect against the risk of outliving savings? Living to a ripe old age would strike most of us as desirable; that is assuming we stay healthy and have sufficient assets to generate enough income to eat.

Risk Pooling

Insurance uses the concept of risk pooling. Golden offers a similar analogy. (35)

If an individual has minimal guaranteed lifetime income, he may rely on his principal and investment gains to sustain himself. Let's assume that this individual has diversified their portfolio and picked stocks in a manner that matches the track-record of the top professionals and oracles in the field without incurring any fees. But of course, he still doesn't know the exact date of death. How can a retiree devise an optimal investment strategy to provide for funds for the duration of life, when one is unable to pinpoint a definite measure of their lifespan?

Stated statistically more formally by Milevsky: "One thing should be absolutely clear: your remaining lifetime is a random variable". (12) In a different book, Milevsky, partnering with Macqueen, suggests an interesting exercise where the reader is invited to record a large sample of random obituaries and observe that range of potential outcomes is fairly high in order to illustrate the point. (36) The key takeaway is that while date of death is unknown for many, it can vary significantly and what the population will experience on average provides minimal insight.

This is similar to automobile insurance where the outcome of incurring damages at the beginning of a policy year is unknown and the average cost of damages for the population having the same car damage risk provides little insight. At the end of the policy year, if the insured did not incur damages, should the insured regret their original purchase of a car insurance policy? I do not believe so and the same reasoning applies to lifetime income or for that matter life insurance.

Conservatism in spending habits in retirement can help retirees decrease their longevity risk. However, this may lead to unnecessarily restricted spending, which places limits on an individual's lifestyle. Further, limiting spending may not be feasible, as some expenses may be unavoidable, such as food and health-related expenses.

Bequest Risk

A common perception of bequest is that it is an issue only the wealthiest individuals in society need to worry about. I believe legacy planning touches anyone who has some assets and does not rely solely on social safety nets for income. Avoiding bequest risk involves striking the right balance between the income a retiree needs and the inheritance they'd like to leave. More specifically, leaving an inheritance that is lower than desired may be unsatisfying. The other side of that coin is that leaving a larger legacy than anticipated, while not a risk per se, could result in limitations on spending that were not necessary and could lead to a reduced lifestyle in retirement. Both scenarios are not desirable. [37]

Unexpected expenses must also be taken into consideration and ideally managed with the right mitigants. LTC issues are typically at the forefront of these types of events in the United States and it is worth noting the medical expenses are one of the leading causes of personal bankruptcies in the United States.

Everyone should have a bequest goal, be it lofty or zero. Having an inheritance strategy that involves "spending whatever amount of assets during retirement and leaving whatever is left behind" is somewhat irrational, unless personal wealth is so significant that the amount spent in retirement will be insignificant relative to an individual's fortune. If leaving an inheritance is a priority, plan accordingly. If leaving a legacy has minimal value for an individual, then it makes sense to maximize assets for the largest possible income during retirement.

Like every other aspect of retirement planning, determining a goal around legacy planning is optimal. Legacy goals will depend on circumstances and personal preferences but whether the objective is to die broke, pass assets to children and later generations or finance several charities, stating the objective helps facilitate appropriate planning. [37] Also, bequest goals may not necessarily be evaluated just in monetary terms. For example, jewelry, family paintings or even a family cottage can be targeted as bequest goals. While those items may have monetary value, they may also have deep sentimental value and leaving those items as a legacy regardless of time of death and monetary value at time of death can be a rational bequest goal.

Bequest risk also includes obligations related to funeral expenses which are important in many societies across the globe. These can be addressed through preneed or final expense insurance products. These types of solutions offer many benefits including personalizing a funeral in advance, access to help at a very emotional time or concierge service options. Others prefer self-funding funeral options. Regardless, it is a noteworthy consideration and the financial implications of this potential burden can have notable financial implications for many.

The bequest dilemma is seen in an example from Caron/Devine from "Bequest goals: more than just an issue for the wealthy":

Example:
"A 65-year-old widowed woman with one son, who is currently 35-year-old, might use the following approach: withdraw funds at a certain rate periodically, such as 4 percent, with a high degree of confidence that this source of income will last until she is 90-year-old. Assuming that future investment performance behaves exactly as planned, many things can happen. Let's look at three different scenarios:

A. The woman passes away at 70-year-old: She would leave a significant bequest.
B. The woman passes away at 90-year-old: She would leave no bequest.
C. The woman passes away at 100-year-old: She would leave no bequest and would have required some financial support prior to that.

Why would it make sense for this woman to leave a significant bequest to her son when he is 40-year-old (scenario A) or no bequest when he is 60-year-old (scenario B)? Scenario C is obviously undesirable and is commonly known as... longevity risk!

From the son's perspective, he faces:
A. A significant bequest in possibly his prime earning years.
B. No bequest when he may start thinking about retirement.
C. A liability while he may be in his retirement." [37]

Should the amount that an individual wishes to leave their heirs rely heavily on the unknown variable of longevity? [37] The above example suggests the opposite. By allocating a certain amount of savings to a lifetime income product, a retiree can better control the size of the legacy they plan to leave behind. [38] If that same individual has no lifetime income, the difference between dying relatively early or late can have a significant financial impact. If they die early, their heirs are more likely to receive a sizable inheritance. On the other hand, a late death might result in a significantly reduced legacy, which is known as bequest risk. In the worst case, an individual may exhaust all their financial resources and end up as a liability to their next of kin; effectively a negative bequest, also known as... longevity risk.

Generally speaking, the more lifetime income a retirement portfolio has, the less bequest will depend on time of death. If the individual with a significant portion of lifetime income dies earlier than expected, the potential inheritance might be less, while if that same individual dies later, the inheritance will likely be larger than expected.

Golden argues that lifetime income is a fair tradeoff for heirs. [39] Pfau and Finke reached similar conclusions in terms of bequest: a survey concluded that the increase in guaranteed income increased the level of confidence of retirees to leave an inheritance as their basic expenses were covered for life. [40] This comes at the expense of leaving a smaller legacy in the event a particular retiree passes away earlier than expected but of course, this information is unknown in advance for healthy retirees.

Comparison to Life Insurance

One way to explain the benefits of owning life insurance is to rationally convey the consequences of not having life insurance. While the probability of dying of a healthy 35-year-old breadwinner is low, it is not zero. The financial consequences of such death on the dependents of that individual could be catastrophic. Putting together the facts that there is a chance that a 35-year-old breadwinner has a risk of dying with the catastrophic impact of that death on their dependents reveals the need and motivation for purchasing life insurance.

A family wage-earner who recognizes their role of providing for their family can appreciate that the unforeseen event of early death might financially impact the entire household. Life insurance can be a very efficient way to manage this risk as through the use of mortality pooling those who live a long time effectively offset the risk of the few who do not and is a good way to protect against that threat. Therefore, purchasing a life insurance policy is generally viewed as a responsible action to take.

On the other hand, buying lifetime income, which is protection against longevity risk, is not necessarily perceived in the same manner. As much as wage-earners see themselves as providers for their family immediately, they often do not picture themselves as a potential liability to their kin a few decades in the future. To further complicate the matter, life insurance premiums are typically low relative to the potential benefit. However, that dynamic is reversed with lifetime income as the contract holders pays a high premium upfront and receives small recurring benefit payments periodically.

Another factor to consider is how the burden of providing for the elderly often creates uncomfortable situations or discussions across generations. Lifetime income can be perceived as money not left as a bequest but lifetime income should be viewed holistically within a portfolio under all living eventualities. [19] These include dying earlier or later than expected. Unfortunately, the benefits of lifetime income to the vast majority of retirees are not nearly as clear cut as the benefits of life or car insurance. Regardless, understanding the benefits of lifetime income is important and the consequences of not integrating it into a retirement portfolio can be high.

Longevity Risk: Who Should be Concerned?

Both longevity risk and bequest risk are issues that should matter to virtually any individual entering retirement, with the exception of the extremes, the poor and the wealthy. Underprivileged people who rely solely on social and public old-age pension programs will likely have no inheritance and no control over longevity risk. Their income will most likely be limited by government set social mechanisms and result in modest spending power. At the other end of the spectrum, very wealthy individuals face little longevity and/or bequest risks. They can often confidently rely on investment income generated by assets to provide for their needs.

Bill Gates for example does not face longevity risk, as the amount of money he will spend during retirement will be a drop in the bucket compared to the amount that will go towards his financial legacy, regardless of how long he lives. However, moving beyond these two extremes, a wide segment of the population is affected by longevity and bequest risks on at least some level and should consider the security and peace of mind, that properly planned lifetime income can bring.

Stated in a more formal way, people who are able to safely generate a periodic investment income of at least the amount they need to live on face little longevity and bequest risk. For example, in a world with no public old-age pension programs or equity markets and only traditional bonds returning 3% risk free, a person worth $1 million can generate $30,000 each year and faces little longevity and bequest risk. That person can live off the investment income generated and leave the principal as an inheritance. While this is merely a rough estimate as there are no guarantees on what the principal will be worth, this view offers a good simple, cursory estimate of the longevity risk exposure faced by an individual. Should the same individual require an annual income exceeding $30,000, he might still face both longevity and bequest risks, as he will need to sell principal throughout retirement, which creates the risk of eventually running out of principal. More formal approaches and exposure guidelines are presented in this book.

This topic has been explored by many, including Vernon with his "magic formula for retirement security": "I > E" where I stands for income and E stands for expenses. [41]

Longevity risk is a key risk for individuals that should not be underestimated. Further, this risk should be approached in tandem with other risks, such as bequest, investment returns, inflation and emergency expense risk. Lifetime income is a key financial vehicle that can facilitate retirement planning and manage longevity risk. Legacies should not be so heavily dependent on time of death. Building solid recurring income during retirement is critical. There is a tradeoff between recurring income while one is alive and leaving a bequest; lifetime income is the only financial tool that can help strike the right balance between income and bequest goals.

III.   Why Now?

*"American workers retiring today
face a more pronounced emphasis on individual
responsibility and risk for their lifetime incomes
than what their parents experienced."*

— AAA Lifetime Income Risk Joint Committee
2013 [18]

Current Environment

Introduction

Why does longevity risk pose such a significant problem? After all, the risks detailed throughout this book are not new. However, longevity risk is becoming a pressing issue for society, as this chapter will explore. Individuals face more responsibility towards their retirement planning today and have much greater longevity risk than their parents a generation ago. [18] [42] [43] Recognizing this, governments and corporations have altered their strategy on assuming large risks — longevity, economic, demographic, health or regulatory — and shifted a significant part of the burden back to individuals.

While the rise in life expectancy increases longevity risk for individuals, the greater risk remains the unknown, just as with any other risk. To help put this in perspective, a good driver is expected to incur less in auto damages than a bad driver, all else being equal but a scenario where a bad driver does not have an accident and a good driver does is not impossible. Both good and bad drivers need to protect themselves against accidents. Carrying this line of reasoning further, people with various health statuses face longevity risk, as an unhealthy person may survive many years and a healthy person may die early.

DB plans and public old-age pension programs can create inter-generational issues, in both in the private and the public sectors. An increase in benefits must be funded and who pays for that increase is not always clear.

Retirees typically lack understanding of many of the financial issues they will face in retirement, especially longevity risk, [18] [44] as well as how it can be mitigated by securing a source of lifetime income. This part will look at the factors contributing to the need to address longevity risk. It will also explore the programs and vehicles associated with lifetime income.

Factors contributing to the need to address longevity risk:
- Unknown time of death
- Technology and advancement in medical science
- Increase in retirement time span
- Uncertain economic environment
- Health care and LTC costs
- Interest rate environment
- Unknown future tax structure
- Spending patterns during retirement

Current programs and vehicles of lifetime income:
- Employer DB Plans
- Government public old-age pension programs
- Private lifetime income products, such as annuities typically sold by insurers

The Purpose and the Environment of Insurance

From the individual perspective, insurance can be viewed as a somewhat unpleasant purchase. Individuals are happy to line up to buy a smartphone or concert tickets, but no such dynamic exists with insurance. Typically, insurance purchases — life, home, auto, LTC etc. — can be triggered by fear, regulation or other cold motivations. This is why life insurance is often referred as a product that is "sold, not bought". [45] Longevity insurance is no exception to the rule.

Let's take a step back and look at why insurance exists in the first place. Brown and Gottlieb identified six characteristics that make a risk insurable: [46]

- It should be economically feasible.
- The economic value of the insurance should be calculable.
- The loss must be definite.
- The loss must be random in nature.
- The exposure in any rate class must be homogeneous.
- Exposure units should be spatially and temporally independent.

Some of the definitions can be counterintuitive as longevity insurance provides benefits when a good outcome occurs; "loss" is survival in this case as opposed to most other types of insurance such as life or car insurance. But all six criteria are defensible in the context of longevity insurance. This suggests that longevity risk is an ideal candidate for insurance and that the presence of annuities or other lifetime income vehicles should be widespread... but they aren't! The annuity puzzle asks the question: What explains the lack of popularity of longevity insurance? Stated more formally, "Economists describe the annuity puzzle as a problem of maximizing lifetime expected utility." [47]

Need to Address Longevity Risk

Unknown Time of Death

As its name denotes, life expectancy is an expected value. While individuals understand it as a broad idea of how long they will live, they are unable to predict where they will fall within on the whole mortality distribution — in other words, when they will die. That distribution is wide as many outcomes — survival length — are possible. [48]

According to the "Social Security Period Life Tables Males 2016", [49] a 65-year-old male is expected to live to age 83. However, an expected value is not a certain indication of when that individual will die. In fact, according to the same assumptions used to determine this life expectancy, that same man at age 65 has only approximately a 4% chance of dying at age 83. Further, that same individual has around a 20% chance of dying between ages 80 to 84. In other words, a 65-year-old man has a 96% chance of not dying at his expected age of death age of 83 and an 80% chance of not dying in his early 80s. While life expectancy is often the primary metric considered by individuals, it is only one piece of the information to be extracted from a distribution. Observing and analyzing the full distribution is necessary.

According to the AAA Longevity Illustrator, there is a 43% chance that a 65-year-old woman of average health will live until at least to age 90. [50] If a group of 100 65-year-old women planned their finances on living to age 90, it is expected that 43 out of the 100 would be in serious financial trouble at an age when returning to the workforce is not an option. Conversely, the other 57 who planned based on living until age 90 but did not survive [36] might have missed out on opportunities to deploy additional capital earlier in their retirement. [51]

Another potential variable to consider is that mortality improvement is uncertain over the course of a few decades. This adds an additional obstacle for individuals attempting to predict how long their retirement will last, as there is a general propensity in the population at misjudging life expectancy. [52]

Technology and Advancement in Science
With computer capabilities reaching new levels every day, it is impossible to project where technology will lead us, especially when it comes to medical advancements. Is a cure for a major disease or a successful preventive approach for a condition suffered by many possible in the medium term? Will this result in a significant increase of life expectancy? The answers may be unknown but the possibilities have the potential to transform needs and risks of retirement.

Increase in Retirement Time Span
Individuals are not only living longer but they have been retiring earlier; at least in the last few decades. [7] As more people spend a greater period of their lives in retirement, their longevity risk exposure increases accordingly. Working longer can mitigate this issue, as it gives more time and flexibility for a pre-retiree to accumulate funds. However, this may not always be a possibility and even if a 60-year-old pre-retiree is willing and capable of working, this may not be an option and therefore a potential risk pre-retirees need to consider.

Continuous Uncertain Economic Environment
The surrounding economic, health, social and demographic environments combined with governmental actions have fueled speculation on the future direction of inflation, interest rates, equity markets and many more. Uncertainty remains around the economic environment, which can cause harm to retirees at a time of vulnerability.

Health Care and LTC Costs

Health care in the United States is expensive. Americans spend more in health care expenses on a per capita basis relative to other industrialized countries. Some governmental programs can help but many individuals are responsible for a non-negligible portion of their health care expenses. Further, health care costs have increased rapidly during the past several decades relative to other industrialized countries as well as inflation. Also, health care costs relative to gross domestic product has been around 17% near the end of the 2010's decade in the United States, compared to a median below 10% for other industrialized countries. This metric is getting close to 20% which has trigger political attention. [53] [54]

Some of those costs are proportional to lifespan such as medication and routine check-ups. Further, there is uncertainty with regards to the future costs of health care, posing a threat to current and future retirees.

Interest Rate Environment

Single Premium Immediate Annuities (SPIA) offer, all else being equal, an expected benefit positively correlated to interest rates. Viewed from this angle, a higher interest rate environment should increase the demand for SPIAs as higher interest rates provide higher benefits. However, a low interest rate environment creates a situation in which fixed income instruments generate lower ongoing income. When translated into dollars of income, for a given amount of principal, a low interest rate environment can be a source of low recurring revenues, hence increasing the demand to generate income from selling assets.

The interest rate environment is therefore a mixed driver of lifetime income. There is a popular argument that SPIAs should not be purchased in a low interest rate environment because interest rates could increase in the future and deferring the purchase of a SPIA for later when interest rates are higher would generate a higher benefit for a given premium, all else being equal. While that is true, over the few decades preceding the time this book is written, interest rates have generally decreased and there is no certainty as to when or if in the future interest rates will again rise. As such, a low interest rate environment should not dissuade an individual from buying lifetime income on that basis alone as in the case of SPIAs, it overlooks the very tangible benefit of mortality pooling in which those who die young provide the benefit for those who live long.

A robust market exists for long-term bonds. If a retiree does not want to lock in a rate of interest for a long time, that decision reflects asset allocation and risk tolerance preferences rather than a situational prevalence of low rates.

Furthermore, other driving assumptions such as mortality can also change. If, for example, there is a cure for a major disease and average longevity rises, the price of a SPIA would increase. That would result in a decrease in the benefit, all else being equal. Buying lifetime income at various points in time in order to extend the economic and mortality timeframe through which lifetime income is bought, akin to "averaging into the stock market with equities", may be a good strategy to reduce risk.

Tax Complexity and Unknown Future Taxes

Future tax rates on ordinary income, capital gains and dividends in decades to come are unknowns. This poses a risk for retirees. Further, the management of tax-sheltered account and various retirement products pose complexity and can have a significant impact on retirement income and wealth. [42]

Further, Forman points out that United States tax treatment on current lifetime income vehicles can also be complex and may have peculiar effects, [55] reiterating the need for tax expertise when considering such products.

Finally, the purchase of lifetime income gets more complex when deciding from which type of account — tax-sheltered or regular account — the purchase should be coming from. Blanchett and Finke pose the question: "Should annuities be purchased from tax-sheltered assets?". [56] The answer requires in-depth analysis.

Programs and Vehicles of Lifetime Income

Three major vehicles currently exist to protect one from longevity risk: DB plans (pension plans offered by employers), governmental benefits offered by mandatory public old-age pension program and guaranteed lifetime income products offered by insurance companies.

In terms of current programs and vehicles of lifetime income, the following reality must be considered:

- Steady decrease in DB Plans
- Public old-age pension program face future uncertainties
- Unpopularity of pure income annuities

We will explore each of those realities but it is important to note the gap between the need and the utilization of what is being offered.

Public Old-Age Pension Programs

Governmental public old-age pension programs are available in most developed countries. In the United States, under Social Security, workers contribute throughout their working lives and the liability of these benefits is borne by the government. The Social Security program in the United States was created in 1935 and as of January 2018, 42.6 million retirees received on average $1,407 a month. [57]

Defined Benefit Pension Plans

Although rapidly decreasing in popularity, some companies still offer DB plans which provide life-contingent payments to their employees throughout retirement. The liability of these benefits is borne by the employer and its providers of capital. If the employer enters bankruptcy, the Pension Benefit Guaranty Corporation in the United States provides protection for workers and retirees.

DB plans have been replaced over time by DC plans. According to Willis Towers Watson, 59% of Fortune 500 employers offered DB plans in 1998; that figure dropped to 16% in 2017. Figure 2 paints a more detailed picture of types of DB plans. [6]

Figure 2: Evolution of DB plans between 1998 - 2017

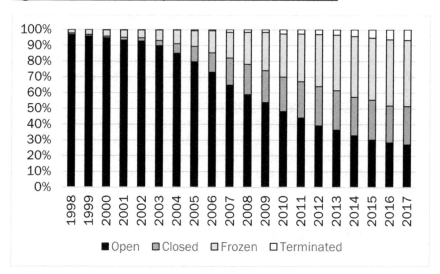

Source: Willis Towers Watson, reproduced with permission [6]

Looking at those facts, one would expect to see demand rise for private lifetime income instruments. However, an SOA paper suggests that this is not the case: "Economic literature has nearly unanimously agreed that, at least from a 'pretax and savings-only' perspective, annuitizing a substantial portion of wealth would enhance the financial welfare of most retirees. The lack of demand in the private annuity market has given rise to a large body of research that attempts to understand the aversion of individuals to annuitization.". [58]

Many factors explain the shift from DB to DC plans. Firms with DB plans struggle with an aging workforce, long-term unpredictability of pension contributions, challenging financial reporting requirements, potential lawsuits, administrative costs, required expertise, dedication of high-level management to focus on DB Plan management and underfunding. These often result from inadequate contributions, volatile investment returns and generally increasing longevity.

Increased scrutiny around the turn of the millennium as to how DB plans were affecting a firm's bottom line or balance sheet strength, combined with declining interest rates, rising longevity — two major drivers of increase in pension liabilities — have all helped to push employers away from DB plans.

But the common explanation that DB plans are simply too expensive is not entirely consistent with the nuances of the situation. First, it is difficult to compare the expenses of DB plans and DC plans on an apples-to-apples basis as the two structures are completely different.

DB plans incur explicit and implicit expenses that DC plans don't incur. It is also difficult to put a price tag on the fact that DB plans can be a form of compensation geared to attract and retain mid-career talent within an organization. It is also unlikely that the perception of expense would adequately explain the ubiquitous shift; pension benefits are part of compensation packages which are dictated by the law of supply and demand.

Both employers and employees have issues with DB plans. The simple lack of general appreciation from the employee's perspective may be a fundamental driving force. Further, DC plan employer contributions are easily identifiable for plan participants, while DB plan employer contributions may not be as observable even if an effort has been made to increase cost transparency over time. Another reason for the interest by individuals in DC plans is the rise of accessibility and affordability of equities and other asset classes through online platforms.

Employees have also found it beneficial to have DB plans phase out as the job landscape itself has changed over the last few generations, with cradle-to-grave employment for a single breadwinner replaced by working families, where individuals changed jobs multiple times over the course of a career. This has caused a decrease in employees' appetite for DB plans. Further, portability issues coupled with inflation and insolvency concerns have also diminished employees desire for DB plans benefits.

Lifetime Income Products

Only a life insurance company can offer the guarantees embedded in a lifetime income products. In the United States, lifetime income products include Single Premium Immediate Annuities (SPIAs), Deferred Income Annuities (DIAs), Variable Annuities (VAs) or Fixed Indexed Annuities (FIAs) with living benefits. In Canada, SPIAs, DIAs and Segregated Funds with living benefits offer similar features and protection.

The purest lifetime income vehicle is the SPIA. VAs and FIAs offer living benefits that are a form of lifetime income. Further, discussions about tontines, Tontine Savings Accounts (TSAs) and Survival Sharing have resurfaced lately and could help retirees in their retirement to provide lifetime income at a lower cost with exposure to various asset classes of their choice. [59]

Section 2, Lifetime Income Vehicles will explore the various product options available.

IV.   The Benefits of Lifetime Income

"Income annuities provide confidence,
the freedom to spend and invest,
as well as the opportunity to leave a legacy."

— Michael Finke
— Wade Pfau, PhD, CFA, RICP
  2019 [40]

Introduction

This chapter explains the benefits of lifetime income-oriented products. In 1998, Milevsky pointed out that "Within the context of annuities (and life insurance), Yaari (1965) and Fischer (1973) [...] demonstrated that in a perfect capital market individuals with no utility of bequest will annuitize all of their marketable wealth." [60] In 2011, Benartzi, Previtero and Thaler stated "We join many other economists who have studied this problem in concluding that many households would benefit by increasing the share of their retirement wealth that is annuitized." [7] Other prominent scholars – including Brown, Horneff, Maurer, Mitchell and Munnell – have put significant energy into conveying the longevity risk narrative. [61] [62] [63] In sum, great minds believe that annuitization can increase individual's financial wealth.

Consumer's Point of View

Decrease Longevity and Bequest Risk

The first goal of lifetime income products is to utilize assets to produce income while an individual is alive. This reduces longevity risk and bequest risk. Lifetime income vehicles such as SPIAs, DIAs, tontines, TSAs or Survival Sharing utilize traditional risk pooling insurance

29

techniques to provide income for as long as contract holders live — which is a great unknown at a very convenient time, while the retiree is alive, as there is a variable cost associated with living.

Benefit at Old Ages

Table 1 shows the IRR for multiple ages of death under the life-only SPIA and life SPIA with 10-year period certain for a $100,00 premium purchased at the age of 65 years old. The benefit for the life-only SPIA is $6,127, while the benefit for the life SPIA with 10-year period certain is $6,000.

Looking at two different ages: 95-year-old and 100-year-old, the IRR for the annuitant who survives to age 95 is 5.0%, while the IRR for the annuitant who survives to age 100 is 5.5%. The difference between the two IRRs is low. For sake of discussion, assume that an individual survives until 95; What is the value of a stream of potentially five payments if he is survives the next five years? Does the 50 basis points (5.5% - 5.0%) difference give justice to this value? At this age, both revenues and expenses are hard to control. Those payments have the potential to avoid depending on a child, grandchild or great grandchild, if such an eventuality is even a possibility. Return on investment is one perspective that should be evaluated but other considerations should also be analyzed, including long-term cash flows at appropriate times.

Table 1: SPIA IRR; Life-Only vs. 10-year Period Certain

Age at Death	Life-Only SPIA	Life SPIA 10-year Period Certain
66	-93.5%	-9.9%
70	-28.6%	-9.9%
74	-9.5%	-9.9%
75	-7.1%	-7.4%
80	-0.3%	-0.5%
85	2.7%	2.4%
90	4.2%	4.0%
95	5.0%	4.8%
100	5.5%	5.4%
105	5.9%	5.7%
110	6.1%	5.9%

As mentioned above, individuals are often too concerned about returns, failing to consider cash flow and protection. The return on investment does not always paint the full picture. Just like in the above example, the value of the last five years of payments cannot be compared with an incremental 50 basis points return.

Returning to the car insurance example, consider whether it makes sense to evaluate a return on car insurance. It's unlikely that individuals buying car insurance assess the results of their car insurance on an investment return basis. For example, an individual buys insurance over one year for $1,000. After one year, if nothing happens to the car, is the policyholder disappointed at the -100% ([$0 – $1,000] / $1,000) return on their insurance policy? On the other hand, if the policyholder crashes their car during the protection period and incurs damages of $11,000, does the individual go brag to his neighbor about his 1,000% ([$11,000 – $1,000] / $1,000) return on his car insurance policy? Most likely not, because he just crashed his car. The point is that insurance is protection and risk pooling. A year later, given that the policyholder did not crash his car, was the decision of getting insurance a bad decision? No, because at that time, the eventuality of crashing the car was an unknown, hence the use of risk pooling. The same rationale applies to income annuities.

Lifetime income is a hybrid between an investment product and an insurance product. Therefore, lifetime income should be analyzed through various lenses.

Inflation

With regards to inflation, SPIAs without inflation protection don't perfectly keep up with inflation. For example, if the purchasing power has decreased by 30% over 20 years, the annuitant of a SPIA is only getting 70 cents of real value for their 20th year SPIA benefit payment relative to its original protection. But without a SPIA, an individual runs the risk of running out of funds if he outlives his savings. So, 70 cents on the dollar while alive, is better than... zero cents on the dollar! At least, with an income annuity, the annuitant is getting a periodic payment.

Further, SPIA benefits at an earlier age allows the annuitant to rely less on the remainder of their portfolio during the early years of retirement. That results in more of the portfolio being available at a later point in time, perhaps when inflation is a real threat.

Figure 3 contrasts the fair value of the SPIA contract with the account balance of a withdrawal method. The fair value of the SPIA is equal to the actuarial present value of future benefits. The actuarial present

31

value was taken from Actuarial Mathematics [64] and contrasted with a systematic withdrawal approach of a fund starting with an opening balance equal to the original premium, withdrawals equal to the life annuity benefit and earning 6% on the balance (6% is the assumption used in the illustrative model in Actuarial Mathematics.).

Figure 3: Fair Value SPIA vs. Withdrawal Method (Alive)

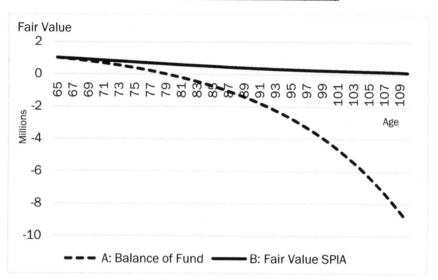

This is a purely academic exercise because prices do not reflect any economic environment and some assumptions are ignored for simplicity and illustration purposes.

Both strategies start with a fair value of $1,000,000. It illustrates two strategies (A and B) for a 65-year-old individual. Each strategy generates the same cash flow amount:

A. Withdraw $101,041 and earn 6% on the balance.
B. Buy a SPIA paying $101,041 while alive.

The fair value of the SPIA (B) decreases but always remains positive, as the annuitant is guaranteed to receive future payments while alive. The fair value of withdrawal method (A) decreases faster as age increases.

The flip side to this chart is that the SPIA (B) fair value is $0 if a person ceased to be alive, while the balance of the fund (A) may be positive in the case of an early death, in this case before age 80.

The important thing to remember is that the fair value of a SPIA while the annuitant is alive will always be greater than the balance of a fund earning the same interest because of mortality credits. Again, the flip side is that the contract is worthless when the annuitant dies.

Inflation is clearly a concern for retirees, which can be addressed by including other asset classes in a portfolio. On the annuity side, inflation can be mitigated through inflation index annuities. However, these products are not always available in every jurisdiction. Another way to reduce inflation risk is to ladder lifetime income starting at various points in time. Through that strategy, on aggregate, payments increase over time, potentially keeping up with inflation. Further a DIA policy can also mitigate inflation risk if combined with a SPIA. A DIA may offer that extra push needed to keep up with inflation in later years. As always, diversification in asset classes is key as there are many unknowns to evaluate as to which asset class will perform better or worse in an inflationary or deflationary environment over the decades spent in retirement.

In the United States, one powerful tool to minimizing longevity risk and inflation risk is to delay Social Security and use assets to fill in the gap years between beginning of retirement and claiming Social Security. This effectively boosts benefits, which are guaranteed for life and have inflation protection. This can help mitigate longevity risk and inflation risk. [18] [65] It has also been suggested that given its appealing characteristics of inflation protection and potential tax advantage, delaying starting to elect the benefit in order to maximize payment amount can be a good strategy, known as "Social Security bridge payment". This essentially sets aside a portion of a retirement portfolio for the sole purpose of creating income for the period of time between one retires and the latest possible time one can elect Social Security. [63] [66] As always, individual situations (especially health status), the economic environment and tax implications need to be assessed by the appropriate professionals.

Recreates Financial Environment Workers are Used to
Most workers have been employed throughout their lives, periodically receiving a paycheck. This creates habits. Some experts believe that recreating this financial environment throughout retirement is desirable, as habits can be hard to change, especially at an older age. [67] Lifetime income reproduces this stream of cash flows.

Increased Freedom with the Remainder of Assets

Purchasing some form of lifetime income provides retirees with recurring income, which allows them to take on more risk, hence potentially higher returns on the balance of their portfolio. If a retiree's entire portfolio is geared towards investments without including any form of annuitization, more caution is required, potentially creating missed opportunities. If an individual relies solely on selling assets in the future to provide for himself, there is the potential exposure to market risk, which can result in a tendency to invest in more conservative investment vehicles. In contrast, having secure recurring income generated by a portion of their portfolio allows a retiree to take on riskier positions with the remainder of their asset base, creating the potential to generate overall higher returns on investment. Inglis, Pfau and Finke seem to reach similar conclusions. [40] [68] [69]

Reduces Dissipation Risk

Dissipation risk is defined by Mettler as "all ways individuals can lose assets after they have been acquired and accumulated". [70] Dissipation risk can occur through personal distress such as illness, lawsuits, loss of employment, divorce or other misfortunes that can not only cause emotional damages but also significant financial damages. Since pure lifetime income has no cash value, it generally cannot be liquidated in the event of personal financial distress; it is an asset that is likely to be the "last-surviving assets" in the event of financial distress. [70]

Reduces Need for Managing Special Situations

While liquidity and optionality are positive investment features for sophisticated investors, those options may not be beneficial for less savvy investors. Further, investment optionality may be costly; investors may not want to pay for features they aren't likely to use.

In addition, professional and institutional investors appreciate liquidity because it facilitates quick conversion of an asset into cash. As such, the flexibility provided by liquidity allows investors to quickly convert the asset into cash to take advantage of another investment opportunity or settle a liability. For retirees, the situation is different because converting assets into cash in order to pay for large purchases such as a new roof or a medical bill removes those assets from the portfolio. That liquidation of retirement assets eliminates the possibility of generating earnings from those assets in the future.

As people age, their ability or interest in managing their finances may decrease. Pure lifetime income usually reduces the need to manage finances. Further, in some cases, other family members may take care of managing finances for an individual, in which case optionality bought in the first place may not be understood well or used properly. As retirees age, an automated financial strategy offers many benefits. [71] Retirees' assets are usually evaluated on a market value basis, so drawing down funds from a portfolio can be a tricky and uncomfortable exercise. This raises questions such as: How much can/should they withdraw in a good return year? in a bad return year?

In these situations, retirees are forced to constantly weigh concerns as to whether they are providing for their current needs and planning properly for retirement. AIM is another approach for considering these issues while offering a strategy to increase spending confidence.

Interest Rate Environment
There is a popular belief that the demand for income annuities is higher in a high interest rate environment. The rationale behind it is that for a given premium, all else being equal, annuity benefits will be higher in a high interest rate environment as opposed to a low interest rate environment. This reasoning is good and mathematically sound. I, however, have a contrarian view on this.

In my view, a low interest rate environment should increase the demand for lifetime income products, all else being equal. A low interest rate environment exacerbates longevity risk. In a high interest rate environment of 10% for example, an individual with capital of $1 million at retirement can produce an annual cash inflow of $100,000 from a fixed-yield investment for life and leave the principal as a bequest. That same strategy in a low interest rate environment, 2% for example, can generate only $20,000 per year. The difference between living with $100,000 or $20,000 is enormous. In a low interest rate environment, all else being equal, retirees should seek methods to draw upon more of their capital; lifetime income is an optimal way to achieve this.

This does not mean that lifetime income should not be used in a high interest rate environment. The same mortality credit mechanism applies, regardless of the interest rate environment. All else being equal, investors investing in a higher interest rate environment will generate more revenues, regardless of the fixed income vehicle they invest in, including bonds or SPIAs.

The idea is not to guess when interest rates will be at a certain level but more to diversify timing of purchase and not letting a low interest rate environment be a sole driver of avoiding SPIAs.

Along those lines, Pfau and Finke brought forward the following equation:

Longer lives + lower interest rates = bonds fall short

Their paper questions the appropriateness of bonds to provide income in a low interest rate environment. [40]

Further, Pfau stated "For someone who has retired, the case for an income annuity actually becomes stronger with low interest rates" somewhat opposing the popular belief that higher interest rates should drive SPIA sales. [72]

Stated in another way, in a world with 0% interest rates, which is not too far off from reality at the time this book is being written, a 65-year-old man with no legacy goals who plans on living on $50,000 per year, requires the following amount of principal depending on his age at death:

- $500,000 if he dies at age 75.
- $1,000,000 if he dies at age 85.
- $2,000,000 if he dies at age 105.

Of course, the main issue is that this man doesn't know in advance when he will die. I therefore believe that the demand for income annuities should be higher in a low interest rate environment because it is more likely a retiree will need an efficient way to deplete their capital.

Changes the Mindset on Longevity Risk

Traditional retirement planning can be done through a systematic withdrawal plan or some sort of fixed income securities vehicle laddering method. [36] Those types of approaches put retirees in a position where they must balance between an income level and a probability of ruin, i.e., longevity risk. The higher the withdrawals are, the higher the chances of running out of funds are and vice versa. By switching a portion of one's savings to lifetime income, that dilemma changes from income vs. longevity risk to income vs. bequest expectation. This will be addressed more formally within the AIM.

Table 2 provides an example of a 65-year-old woman with $1 million who can only invest in long-term bonds and SPIAs. In this scenario, long-term bond rates are 3% and SPIA payout rates are 7%. Income is generated from the yield and the payout of the SPIA. Looking at the two extreme allocations:

Table 2: Bond and SPIA Extremes; Income vs. Bequest

Allocation	Yearly Income	Estimated Bequest
100% in bonds	$30,000	$1,000,000
100% in SPIA	$70,000	$0

These amounts are independent of time of death. Recurring income and estimated legacy can be calibrated by changing the allocation to bonds or SPIAs. For example, if a retiree wanted to do a 50/50 allocation, the yearly income would be $50,000 with an expected inheritance of $500,000.

Table 3: Bond and SPIA Split; Income vs. Bequest

Bond Allocation	SPIA Allocation	Yearly Income	Estimated Bequest
100%	0%	$30,000	$1,000,000
75%	25%	$40,000	$750,000
50%	50%	$50,000	$500,000
25%	75%	$60,000	$250,000
0%	100%	$70,000	$0

This dynamic allows the retiree to avoid guessing their age of death or heavily depending on major assumptions on future investment performance.

In contrast, if that same individual used a systematic withdrawal plan method, the income vs. bequest dynamic is replaced with a spending vs. probability of ruin dynamic. Under a systematic withdrawal plan method, this same individual earns returns equal to the rate from fixed income instruments. This woman faces the following dilemma: the higher the withdrawals, the higher her probability of running out of funds is. For example, if she withdraws $70,000 per year, she will run out of funds if she makes it to 84. If she goes for a more conservative route and withdraws $50,000 per year, she will run out of money only at 96. Further, her legacy will significantly depend on when she passes away. If she dies early on in retirement, her legacy will be larger. However, if she dies at an older age, the legacy will be reduced substantially. Bequest can even be negative, i.e., living expenses covered by family members which is longevity risk. Spending rates come at the expense of a higher probability of ruin. Lifetime income can change that dynamic.

Increase Satisfaction and Happiness

A study conducted among British citizens links the presence of lifetime income and happiness. [73] Other research suggests that retirees' satisfaction increases as guaranteed income increases. More specifically, Finke and Pfau note that retirees' sense of confidence and freedom rise as a result of purchasing an income annuity. In addition, income annuities allow retirees to increase risk exposure with the remainder of their portfolio and also gain security with regards to legacy. This result was observed in a survey performed by the University of Michigan on 20,000 older Americans. [40]

2. Lifetime Income Vehicles

V.   Annuities

"Annuities are pretty simple when you can clear away all the technicalities and legalities."

— Kerry Pechter
2008 [74]

Annuities in General

The word annuity is very confusing. In the United States, it refers to many different types of financial vehicles trying to achieve various objectives. [75] The terminology annuity refers to an insurance product. In its purest form, an annuity is a stream of payments. Lexico, powered by Oxford defines the term annuity as "A fixed sum of money paid to someone each year, typically for the rest of their life". The word comes from the Latin word "annuitas". [76] In 27 B.C., Romans were using these types of contracts in which contract holders payed an upfront premium in return for a stream of payments. [38] In the current United States marketplace, annuities are offered in multiple flavors, serve very different purposes and can be used both in the accumulation and the decumulation phases of retirement.

The terminology can get confusing for advisors, practitioners and academics across different practices and countries. Needless to say, retirees can also get confused. Within the decumulation phase, SPIAs, DIAs, FIAs and VAs with living benefits represent lifetime income. While annuities in general haven't gained widespread acceptance, SPIAs and DIAs in particular have not been popular. Advisors, practitioners and academics have long studied the lack of popularity of income annuities and other longevity risk products in the marketplace. As of the writing

41

of this book, lifetime income products are under-utilized. [7] [38] [62] [77] Milevsky offers a great literature review with regards to the annuity puzzle in "Life Annuities: An Optimal Product for Retirement Income". [16] According to a study performed by Greenwald & Associates and CANNEX, consumers continue to believe that annuities:

- Have too many terms and conditions.
- Hinder their access to their money.
- Are difficult to understand. [78]

While VAs with living benefits may have many terms and conditions, SPIAs are fairly straight-forward contracts. SPIAs do restrict the access of contract holders to their money; however, this condition is essential for insurers to continue to pay out income based on the necessary financial mortality credit mechanism. At the same time, a fixed deferred annuity (FDA) provides ample access to funds after the surrender charge period is over but SPIAs and FDAs are designed to provide income under completely separate circumstances. While they are both called annuities and are both financial vehicles, it makes little sense to compare and contrast the two.

VI. Demystifying SPIAs and DIAs

"SPIAs are simple and elegant financial products [...] and have withstood the passing of over a thousand years."

— Gary Mettler, CFP, CEBS
2014 [70]

Introduction

SPIAs and DIAs Now and Yesterday

SPIAs have existed for a few millennia, yet they are still not well understood nor appreciated by the general public. They are known as life annuities (rentes viagères in French) in Canada. Their lack of popularity is striking at a time when the use of DB plans is significantly declining. Rising longevity will mean that people face a much longer retirement than past generations. This book will explore why, despite some purchase concerns, SPIAs are an extremely important strategic tool in sound retirement planning. This chapter will examine them from an IRR and cash flow perspective and show how they are one of the very few financial vehicles that can deal with the simple fact that a retiree does not know in advance how long he/she will live. This chapter will also examine Deferred Income Annuities (DIAs) or Qualified Longevity Annuity Contracts (QLACs), a close cousin of SPIAs.

Preliminary Specifications

Single Premium Immediate Annuities

The simplest form of guaranteed lifetime income is offered through a product called a single premium immediate annuity (SPIA). The terms are simple: SPIAs are insurance contracts where the contract holder (the owner of the contract) pays a single premium to the insurance company in exchange for recurring benefit payments while the contract holder is alive. SPIAs effectively buy retirees a traditional DB pension. For example, a male age 65 could pay $10,000 and receive $53 per month for the rest of his life. The main variables driving SPIA prices are mortality rates and interest rates. SPIAs come in many flavors but unless otherwise specified, SPIAs referred in this book are life-only SPIAs, which means that they include no period certain or other survivor benefits. Due to those parameters, these instruments will be referred to as pure SPIAs.

The difference between a SPIA and a traditional life insurance policy is that the latter financially protects the insured from the risk of the cost of premature death, whereas the SPIA is intended to do just the opposite by offering protection from the financial consequences of extended longevity. Put another way, life insurance is intended to provide financial protection from dying too soon, whereas a SPIA provides insurance against living too long.

Internal Rate of Return

The ratio of the benefit payment to the premium is referred to as the payout rate. [79] It should not be confused with the yield or the IRR reported on a typical fixed income instrument such as a bond. The IRR on a SPIA can be calculated but only once the contract is over, which is when the annuitant dies. Since benefit payments are paid as long as the annuitant lives, the timing of death impacts the IRR.

The comparison of a SPIA to a long-term bond can be misleading. While there are similarities between the two, there is a major caveat to this view: the SPIA owner doesn't receive the face value at the end of the period/life. The payout rate on a SPIA (calculated as [Yearly Annuity Payment] / [Initial Premium]) should be greater than the yield from a long-term bond (calculated as the IRR of the bond) of similar credit quality. That's because each benefit payment includes mortality credits, interest and return of principal payment, which provides significant income leverage in comparison to long-term bonds. The typical bond will return the face amount at the end of a pre-determined period, while the pure SPIA will return nothing at the end of the annuitant's life. Effectively, in a SPIA, the principal is returned partially through each benefit payment.

Insurance companies typically use a conservative asset portfolio to support future benefit payments and thus to price SPIAs and DIAs. Coupled with risk pooling, carriers can offer lifetime income products and provide a mechanism such that individuals who live longer get subsidized by the ones who die earlier.

Mortality Credits

Many authors have offered definitions and attributes of mortality credits with their respective nuances (including but not limited to Milevsky, Dellinger, Mettler and Hegna [16] [20] [38] [70]). Mortality credits are the part of the benefit paid to compensate SPIA contract holders for foregoing their principal upon death. Annuitants give up the remainder of their theoretical account balance upon death. In effect, mortality credits are a solving mechanism such that each payment to the annuitant is equal, while also ensuring that each contract is actuarially sound. Mortality credits accomplish their purpose by redirecting the assumed principal of deceased annuitants to surviving annuitants. It is this risk pooling mechanism through which insurance companies redistribute principal from contract holders who pass away early to those who live longer. These calculations are structured on interest, principal consumption and mortality credits, so that payments remain level through the life of the contract. This risk pooling mechanism is used in all other types of insurance. For example, in car insurance, the insurance company collects premiums from many automobile drivers and applies most of it to the drivers who incurred an accident. Mortality credits are the element that boosts IRR for annuitants who live longer and allows the carrier to pay a larger fixed dollar amount of recurring benefits to annuitants, relative to fixed income securities of similar credit quality. Contract holders don't necessarily need to understand this mechanism and it changes nothing to the simple contractual agreement in a SPIA.

Contractually, in a SPIA contract, the contract holder pays a lump sum premium to the insurance company in exchange for a series of payments while the contract holder is alive. Contract holders most likely won't technically view the components of each of their payments but each benefit payment consists of:

- Return of principal.
- Interest on that principal balance.
- Mortality credits.

For the first two components — return of principal and interest on the principal balance — most people are typically familiar with this concept because it relates to how mortgages are structured. However, the process is reversed from the way a mortgage typically works as the annuitant pays the lump sum upfront and receives the monthly payments. The third component to the payment is the mortality credits. Mortality credits allow individuals to benefit from a financial vehicle that pays income throughout their life. This feature of annuities removes at least some of the risk associated with longevity.

Mortality Credit Example

In order to illustrate the concept of mortality credit, let's go back a few millennia and explore the practice of decimation used by the Roman army. Decimation is a military discipline measure — rather extreme, morbid and barbaric — but one that perfectly illustrates the concept of mortality credits. The practice consists of executing one out of 10 soldiers of a particular cohort, typically containing several hundreds of soldiers, due to a capital offense committed by the particular unit. [80] In other words, a cohort containing a large number of soldiers was facing the following punishment: every member had a one out of 10 chance of being executed. Now, imagine 100 combatants from a unit facing this situation; it is expected that 90 of the 100 combatants will come back alive from the decimation. Knowing this in advance, a subgroup of 100 Roman soldiers from this unit each put in 10 pieces of gold in a chest such that the box contains 1,000 pieces of gold. The chest is a securely stored and generates no investment returns and incurs no storage costs. The 100 combatants agree to split evenly the funds among all survivors after the decimation is completed.

Once that is done, as expected, 10 soldiers from the group pass away. The other 90 members of the subgroup are alive; they open the chest. Since all members contributed to the fund equally, they split evenly the proceeds of the fund hence 11.11 pieces of gold each — the sum which remains when 1,000 pieces of gold are divided by 90 soldiers. Each surviving soldier effectively made a 11.11% return on their investment or 11.11 pieces of gold out of the original 10 pieces of gold, while the deceased member had a -100% return on its investment, as the deceased member originally put in 10 pieces of gold and received nothing back. The 1.11 gain for each surviving member comes from the deceased member's initial investment split among all 90 surviving members — 10 pieces of gold x 10 soldiers / 90 soldiers = 1.11 pieces of gold. From the perspective of our discussion on annuities and mortality credits, consider the 1.11 as a mortality credit because it is the amount by which each surviving member was compensated by agreeing to forego their principal upon death. If all 100 members came back alive, the return on investment of each member would have been 0%, while if only 80 members would have come back alive, each surviving member would have earned a 25% return on their investment, boosted by the other 20 members who would have forfeited their original investment. Mettler and Milevsky among others have brought forward such explanations on mortality credits. [70] [81]

Comparison to Mortgage

A SPIA can be thought of, mechanically, as a mortgage but with two fundamental differences.

First, in a typical mortgage contract, a financial institution provides an initial cash outflow in exchange for a series of future payments. In a typical SPIA contract, an individual provides the initial cash outflow in exchange for a series of future payments made by a financial institution.

Second, for both mortgages and SPIAs, payments consist of a return of principal and interest paid on the balance but for the SPIA, there is an additional component: mortality credits.

Table 4: Mortgage vs. SPIA

		Mortgage	SPIA
Receives	Initial cash outflow	Individual	Financial firm
	Periodical payments	Financial firm	Individual
Payment consist of	Return of principal	Yes	Yes*
	Interest on balance	Yes	Yes
	Mortality credit	No	Yes
Position of individual	While alive	Owe balance	Get payments
	Upon death	Owe balance	Nothing

*forgo at death

Pricing

From an insurer's perspective, the pricing exercise needs to take into consideration several factors including:

- Expected future benefits based on assumed mortality.
- Reserves that need to be held to support future benefit payments.
- The earned rate on the assets backing the reserves.
- The expenses incurred in manufacturing the product including salaries and commissions to administer and sell the product.
- Capital requirements necessary to satisfy regulatory and rating agencies requirements to offer the product, which needs to be taken into account in the pricing exercise.
- Profit the insurance company expects to return to its providers of capital who are ultimately responsible for the liability incurred and are taking a risk for which they expect to be compensated.

Further, sensitivity, stress and scenario testing are essential on the annuities as a standalone operation, as well as enterprise wide. Mortality rates and earned rates are usually the primary variables tested. The impact and potential mitigation from other lines of businesses must also be considered.

Various considerations also need to be put into place regarding different product features, such as a period certain. A period certain feature under a SPIA stipulates that annuity benefits are paid for the period certain if the contract holder dies before the end of the period certain.

Just as with virtually any other type of insurance contract, insurance companies pool many of these contracts and uses the law of large numbers to reduce risk and offer a product at a reasonable price. Dellinger provides a well-articulated detailed explanation of the mechanics behind annuities in his book "The Handbook of Variable Income Annuities". [38]

Insurance companies leverage their investment and risk pooling capabilities to offer SPIAs. The law of large numbers stipulates that "as the number of identically distributed, randomly generated variables increases, their sample mean (average) approaches their theoretical mean." [82] In insurance, this means that as the number of policyholders rises, the predictability of the outcome for that group of policyholders will also increase. With a SPIA, some annuitants will die before the end of their expected lifespan while others will die after the end of their expected lifespan. All annuitants will get a payout as long as they live due to the mortality credit mechanism employed by insurance companies.

Anti-Selection

While the longevity risk facing individuals in good health may be obvious, the longevity risk facing individuals in poorer health cannot be ignored. This matters because current lifetime income products aren't an attractive solution for those in poor health. That's because they are priced using assumptions for the entire pool with no differentiation based on health of other factors. This leads to the logical conclusion that unhealthy retirees should not buy SPIAs unless they are underwritten.

Health also plays an important role in the purchase of lifetime income. Significantly impaired individuals should not purchase lifetime income unless it is underwritten as it would not be in their financial interest to do so. Underwritten SPIAs are not popular in the United States. [83]

Insurers take into consideration that purchasers of SPIAs may be healthier than the average population. This creates a dynamic where benefits for a given premium may not be that attractive to a significant portion of the population. With the rise of longevity risk, coupled with technological improvements, underwriting capabilities and efficiencies could improve and change this dynamic in the future, allowing SPIAs to be available to a broader portion of the population.

Deferred Income Annuity

DIAs or QLACs are contracts where the contract holder pays the insurance company a lump sum upfront in return for a stream of annuity benefit payments starting at a later date. Those payments will occur for the remainder of the individual's life.

DIAs work like SPIAs with the exception that annuity benefits start at a later date, as opposed to immediately, as SPIAs do. DIAs in their purest form do not provide any benefit during the deferral phase but some do offer death benefits.

DIAs offer a potential alternative to hedge longevity risk that may be within the financial reach of a far greater number of retirees. Essentially, they provide lifetime payouts, just like a SPIA but these do not begin until a later age, typically 80 or 85. In the United States, special laws allow individuals to contribute a certain amount from their tax deferred retirement savings vehicle to postpone required minimum distribution (RMD). Relative to traditional SPIAs, their purchase results in a much larger benefit for a given premium. For example, a QLAC purchased at age 65 for a male could offer a lifetime annual payout of benefits in the order of magnitude of a quarter of the original premium if these commenced at age 80 or about half if they began at age 85. A SPIA starting immediately would result in a lifetime annual payout in the mid-single digits. While the difference between starting benefits at age 80 or 85 result in a significant difference, the difference in probabilities of getting those benefits is also substantial.

DIAs can also be used as an inflation mitigator, as the contract holder pays an upfront premium in exchange for higher benefits at a later point in life. While the pattern of benefit payments is typically level, DIA benefits are funds coming at a later point in life where cumulative inflation may have eroded a retiree's purchasing power.

The DIA deferral period elected might be 15 or 20 years. A SPIA is effectively a DIA with no or little deferral period.

Fixed Deferred Annuity

While DIAs and FDAs are both annuities, in practice they are quite different. Contractually, the main difference between a DIA and a FDA is that the annuitization or conversion of a lump sum in lifetime income at the end of the deferral period is mandatory and pre-determined for a DIA, while it's a possibility for an FDA. Also, the FDA has a cash value that accumulates over time. In contrast, a DIA has no cash value and it is strictly a promise of payments. Historically, annuitization rates, which represent the proportion of FDA annuitants annuitizing their funds, have been very low. [84] FDA, despite the inclusion of the word annuity in the term, are mainly accumulation-type products, competing mainly against bank CDs and bonds. Further, FDA annuitants benefit from favorable tax treatments, compared to other saving-oriented vehicles. In contrast, DIAs offer longevity protection and automatically convert lump sums into lifetime income. DIAs may or may not offer a death benefit in case of death during the deferred phase. A DIA with no death benefit during the deferral phase will result in a higher annuity benefit in the payout phase, all else being equal.

SPIAs and DIAs are vastly different from traditional FDAs. Table 5 summarizes those differences:

Table 5: Deferred Annuity; Accumulation vs. Income

	FDA	DIA
Retirement Phase	Accumulation	Decumulation
Annuitization	Optional	Mandatory
Annuitization terms	At annuitization date	At issue date
Benefits at death:		
Accumulation	Premium + interest	0
Decumulation	0	0
Annuity benefits	Much lower	Much higher
Main purpose	Tax deferred growth	Longevity protection

Issues and Misconception on SPIAs and DIAs

Investment, Insurance or Both?

SPIAs and DIAs are hybrid financial instruments that operate in a zone between investment and insurance products. The hybrid nature of SPIAs inherently creates a great deal of misunderstanding as to how they should be valued relative to other types of investments. Essentially, SPIAs are a cross between a traditional fixed income investment and insurance protection.

The worlds of investments and insurance can be complex from a manufacturing and a distribution perspective. While this book does not address these ramifications in the various jurisdictions, it is interesting to point out that it is a sensitive issue, especially in the United States. For example, Michelle Richter recently formed Fiduciary Insurance Services, LLC to tackle those issues, illustrating the complexity of both the insurance and the investment environments. Richter points that "I want to help those advisers who are not insurance experts and those insurance experts who are not investment product experts, to develop programmatic intellectual frameworks that intelligently weave together products for systematic solutions to common consumer challenges". [85] This alone signals the need to bridge the gap between the investment and insurance thinking, as both worlds have some much in common, yet tend to be miles apart in actuality.

Insurance View

Contractually, a SPIA is an insurance product. It is protection oriented in the sense that a contract holder pays a premium in exchange for future recurring benefits triggered by a specific event, in this case, surviving. It may be counterintuitive to think about SPIAs as insurance because in general, insurance contracts for other products such as life, home or auto are structured in a way that the contract holder pays a small premium relative to the potential benefits. These products also operate on the basis of a low probability of occurrence and high severity. Lifetime income works somewhat the other way around; the contract holder pays a hefty premium upfront and expects to receive recurring small benefits. For example, with home insurance, homeowners typically pay a small premium relative to the potential benefit they may receive in the unlikely event that a fire burns down their house. In truth, most of those with homeowners' insurance will never suffer through a fire or other catastrophe. However, the few that do will be covered by insurance to recompense them for their loss.

In contrast to the popular conception of a traditional insurance products, SPIA contracts are designed to protect individuals from what is generally viewed by society as a positive event — a longer life. This contrasts with other typical types of insurance, where insurance is aimed at providing financial protection against undesirable events such as car accidents or death; something bad happens but insurance is present to compensate the financial loss associated with the unforeseen event. Longevity insurance is the opposite: the longer the annuitant lives, the larger the cumulative payout is, which is a double positive in the event of a long life. The converse holds true: it's a double negative if the annuitant dies early.

Investment View
SPIAs also have an investment flavor in the sense that individuals put up an initial amount — the premium — with the expectation and hope that they will receive back through time more than that initial outlay. A SPIA purchase has high downside risk in the event the annuitant dies earlier than expected and has no death benefit. At the same time, it offers a compensating upside in the event the annuitant lives longer than average in terms of return on that investment. This is not an intuitive way to think about investments, as investors usually have in mind a different risk reward expectation. But this doesn't mean it is a bad financial arrangement as the likelihood of incurring a significantly negative return is low. Further, returns and cash flows received are correlated in a fashion that corresponds to an individual's income need; while they are alive.

Potential Significant Losses on SPIAs
Since there are no bequest prospects because of a lack of return of premium, pre-retirees fear losing estate value at the time of death if

they purchase a SPIA. From either a dollar amount or IRR perspective, an early death on a SPIA may result in a very undesirable scenario. Pre-retirees can partially mitigate this risk by electing a death benefit, also known as return of premium or period certain but this comes at a cost. This cost is a lower ongoing benefit or monthly payment.

Part of the lack of comfort in SPIAs may be due to the very conservative label attached to it. Retirees can also potentially see the product as very risky from a different perspective: an early death. In the event of a SPIA purchase at age 65 and an early death, say at age 70, the return on the financial vehicle may be worse than -25% for a five-year period. Not a glorious return on investment, which is why it is important to understand every facet and every eventuality before purchasing a SPIA. Also, it's important to keep in mind that the eventuality of an early death is associated with a low probability.

Lack of Perceived Tangibility

Technically, all financial securities are non-material or abstract, considered impalpable. That's because unlike other assets, such as real estate, fine art or gold coins, you can't touch securities or shares of a fund. Previously, many people held individual stock or bond certificates in a safety deposit box or home safe. However, that practice has largely disappeared with the advent of the internet and online securities custodians. This means that financial instruments are now money transfers, words and numbers written on a piece of paper or a website with an account value. It is perhaps even more difficult to place a value on are SPIAs, as they don't have an associated account value and they don't support annual reporting statements or even periodic mark-to-market valuations.

This further contrasts with mutual fund type accounts as those financial vehicles provide an account value, while SPIAs don't, just like car insurance. They do, however, have a fair value.

For most young workers, their largest financial asset is their future earning power; there is no account value for that. Seen in that context, the concept of generating earnings without an account value associated to it is not entirely foreign.

SPIAs can be perceived as both an investment or insurance and the value and risk reward tradeoff can be hard to explain to potential clients. [8]

Irreversibility

Once a SPIA is purchased, it is irreversible (except for a brief free-look period). This means that once the contract is issued, it cannot be cancelled; the contract holder receives its benefits and does not have to put in extra premiums. This design is necessary in order for the risk pooling mechanism to function adequately. There is no way around it, just like a contract holder cannot get its premium back after a year of home insurance coverage. An individual can always buy more SPIAs through separate contracts but once a single policy is purchased, it is locked and the contract holder only collects the benefits while alive.

Credit Risk

Rating agencies have sophisticated methodologies to assess issuers' ability to pay future claims. These ratings are available to consumers and are a powerful tool to assess the appropriateness of a purchase. From a consumer's perspective, for a given combination of premium and benefits, a potential buyer is better off with a higher rating, as the likelihood of making good on the promise is higher with a higher rating. Diversification among various issuers is also key, as a default in one issuer may not be as dramatic if the retirees owns multiple SPIA contracts from various issuers.

Expensive

SPIAs are indeed expensive due to the administrative and selling expenses. Further, regulators and rating agencies may impose significant reserves and capital behind policies in order to protect the general public, which also contributes to the cost. Lastly, providers of capital to insurance companies expect to be compensated for the risk they undertake, which is ultimately paid by the contract holder. Sabin estimates "that insurers typically charge a premium that is 14% higher than fair." [86] That 14% is an estimate for the expenses and profits above the pure actuarial value of the benefits. Having said that, this dynamic is mainly true for virtually all insurance products. This does not necessarily mean that the purchase of such products is a bad idea; insurance companies are in the business of risk pooling. Building that infrastructure requires expenses and expected profits. Those factors impact the ultimate price of lifetime income products, just as expense inputs affect pricing in other industries.

Risk Far in the Future

Insurance products usually provide protection against an immediate threat. For example, homeowners usually insure themselves against a fire, if the event occurs within the next year. The same dynamic holds true for life insurance. Longevity insurance protects individuals against a risk that is far in the future — perhaps as far as many decades.

This does not mean that the risk is not present. Acting to mitigate longevity risk as early as possible in life is a viable strategy because individuals tend to have more flexibility earlier rather than later. For example, a person close to retirement may have the possibility to work a little longer to save more and start depleting its retirement assets later, in contrast to someone who has been retired for 15 years for whom going back to work may most likely not be possible.

Slow Bleeding Risk

In reality, waking up one day and having no money after spending funds in a confident way is an unlikely outcome. A more likely outcome is a situation in which individuals reach an older age with a reduced amount of income and assets than anticipated. In this case, most of these individuals will then slowly decrease their spending. While this is less potentially catastrophic than a spectacular accident such as a car wreck or a death of a family wage earner, it does not diminish specific longevity risk. [87] This is especially true if this situation occurs in the context of rising health care expenses associated with limitations on activities of daily living. Spending on personal care attendants or assisted living can quickly exhaust income-producing assets, which is another argument in favor of lifetime income products.

Absence of Related Threat

For many reasons outlined in this book, longevity risk was less present a generation ago, as individuals did not usually experience a 30-year retirement and, in any case, were usually covered by DB plans. Few people have seen their parents, friends or family facing longevity risk. [18] [38] People who have lived through or seen catastrophic events tend to be more sensitive about such issues. As society experiences the first generation of retirees who are living longer without the benefit of DB plans, hopefully awareness around this critical issue will increase, prompting society at large and individual families to take steps to mitigate these issues.

All or Nothing Perception

As soon as the word annuitization appears in someone's mind, the thought of dying early and losing everything follows. [16] In reality, annuitization is not necessarily appropriate for all the assets in an individual's portfolio. In fact, many experts recommend purchasing a portfolio of income generating products slowly across various economic environments. Adapting a diversified portfolio to the needs that arise over the entire lifecycle of a retirement can be a productive strategy.

VII.   Real Life Example

"There are two aspects to addressing longevity [...]
First, understanding it and then planning an income
that will last throughout life."

— Noel Abkemeier, FSA, MAAA
2016 [88]

This chapter will refer to a typical individual considering the purchase of a SPIA as part of a portfolio. This is an illustrative example with hypothetical data and does not consist of a recommendation.

Meet Mike

Mike has the following characteristics:

- Gender: Male
- Age: 65.0 years old
- Health: Good
- SPIA:
  - Frequency: Yearly
  - 1st payment: Immediately

Scenarios

Looking at three different scenarios, Mike pays a premium at age 65 and receives annual annuity benefit payments depending on his age of death, as illustrated in Table 6.

Table 6: Annuity Payments at Various Ages of Death

Scenarios	Death Age	Number of Annual Annuity Payments
A	75.5	11
B	85.5	21
C	95.5	31

In each scenario, Mike buys a SPIA and a treasury bond of the same dollar amount with bond maturity corresponding to his remaining life span. The bond is held until maturity. Of course, Mike does not know this in advance but this comparison is done to illustrate the SPIA mechanics from a return perspective. This comparison removes all bias as financial instruments are readily available at market prices. It also removes the need to make assumptions on future market environments such as putting a price on the 20-year bond 10 years from now that would require assumptions. Returns are calculated and presented treating the individual and his estate as one entity.

Numerical Results

This segment provides a few numerical examples.

Table 7: Market Entries

Scenarios	Death Age	Bond Yield	SPIA Rate
A	75	1.57%	6.13%
B	85	1.90%	6.13%
C	95	2.29%	6.13%

Table 8: IRR on Investment

Scenarios	Death Age	Bond IRR	SPIA IRR
A	75	1.57%	-7.09%
B	85	1.90%	2.68%
C	95	2.29%	5.03%

Table 9: Annual Revenues from $1 million Investment

Scenarios	Death Age	Bond Revenues	SPIA Revenues
A	75	$15,700	$61,270
B	85	$19,000	$61,270
C	95	$22,900	$61,270

Table 10: Bequest from $1 million Investment

Scenarios	Death Age	Bond Bequest	SPIA Bequest
All	All	$1,000,000	$0

Key Conclusions

A few key conclusions can be drawn from the above tables:

- The IRR for a SPIA increases as the annuitant lives longer, while the timing of death in no way affects the IRR on a bond. The bond yield increasing with age in Table 8 is a result of the positive yield curve slope of the illustrative example.
- Early death can lead to negative return on investment for a SPIA if there are no death benefits. A SPIA purchase results in high recurring income dollars and no bequest.
- The bond purchase results in low recurring income dollars and a legacy equal to the initial purchase.
- The returns on investment of the SPIA and the bond for the approximate life expectancy — 20 years in this case — are of the same order of magnitude, specifically 2.68% for the SPIA vs. 1.90% for the bond.

US Treasuries and SPIAs: Credit and Liquidity

The tables above compare promised returns from private carriers to U.S. treasury returns. From a credit perspective, the government backed bond is more secure; however, SPIAs are also very secure. I believe the comparison is fair. The AAA Lifetime Income Risk Joint Committee rates "Insured Solutions" which includes SPIAs as "Exceptional", with a grade of 4 out of 4 in the "Credit Risk/Market Risk Protection" category. [89] Consumers can address credit concerns on SPIAs by relying on issuer's credit ratings of companies issuing the product. Further, diversifying across various issuers can help dissipate the concentration in credit risk. Further, government back guaranty associations exist in many jurisdictions.

Bonds are very liquid assets while SPIAs are significantly less liquid. While bond liquidity is a beneficial feature, it is important to remember if the liquidity aspect of the bond is utilized — that is, all or part of it is sold — at least some of the value and earning power of the bond will be depleted. However, if funds are reinvested, it could allow Mike to invest in other opportunities.

VIII.   Annuity Benefits

"The nastiest, hardest problem in finance."
(referring to *"decumulation*
or the use of savings in retirement")

—   William Sharpe, 1990 Nobel Prize Laureate in Economics
2017 [90]

Matches Expenses

There is a variable cost associated with living because people spend money while they are alive. SPIAs provide benefits while annuitants are alive through the mechanism of a natural paycheck replacement. Eating, housing, traveling, healthcare or clothing expenses to name a few are all expenses incurred while an individual is alive. SPIAs provide spending confidence to annuitants as the benefit payments continue as long as the annuitant is alive. It's the closest financial instrument to a paycheck. In fact, it's even better than a paycheck, as SPIAs don't typically lay-off or fire annuitants. The analogy of getting fired from employment to annuities would be a default from the carrier, which is not impossible. Retirees can mitigate this risk by purchasing annuities from high rated carriers. Further, retirees can diversify across various annuity providers to mitigate that loss. It is typically difficult to achieve this through employment, i.e. having multiple jobs.

SPIAs for Longevity and Bequest Risk

SPIAs help retirees manage their bequest goals and make financial planning less dependent on their time of death. [37] In a very simplistic scenario where Mike has $1 million and has to pick between buying the 20-year bond or the SPIA (looking at scenario B in prior chapter, for example), the SPIA would provide recurring income of $61,000 per year and $0 at death while the bond would provide recurring income of $19,000 per year and $1 million at death. Which one is preferable? In the above example, splitting the above $1 million portfolio half and half would result in a $40,000 yearly revenue and a $500,000 legacy, regardless of time of death. Retirees should not choose between income or bequest. Instead, they should seek an appropriate balance between the two.

Effect on the Remaining Portfolio

A SPIA secures recurring payments in an effective way as it combines return of principal, interest income and risk pooling enhancements in one recurring benefit payment without market risk exposure. Combined with Social Security and possibly a DB pension as well as investment income generated by the remainder of a retiree portfolio, it provides a solid basis for a paycheck replacement during retirement. This allows retirees to manage the rest of their portfolio in a more opportunistic and strategic approach instead of being forced to liquidate assets periodically to fund recurring needs. If a retiree wants to take more risks through equity or real estate exposure, the retiree can do so with the knowledge that ongoing recurring reliable income. Alternatively, the retiree can lock in gains from other investments at a time that is not necessarily dictated by the need to provide for basic living expenses. Investors always want to be in a position of strength so that they aren't forced to sell assets at a specific time. SPIAs facilitate that ability to be in control. Further, SPIA payments are designed to be spent but individuals aren't obligated to spend their benefit payments; instead, they could reinvest these payments in an investment portfolio if there is excess income.

Insurance Value

Consumers can generally gain comfort from the experience of executing a purchase through its entire life. For example, buying a house, living in it for a while and selling it can help individuals gain comfort in a subsequent home purchase. SPIAs are tricky because consumers will never go through a full circle of a SPIA purchase and gain that perspective, as the benefits of a SPIA end with death. It may be natural to compare SPIAs with other financial instruments and focus on aspects such as liquidity, return on investment, tradability or volatility. Those characteristics don't necessarily translate well when evaluating SPIAs. Some consumers who are not familiar with the value proposition of insurance may dismiss them as poor investments. That's because these consumers lack the ability to weigh the value of the insurance and risk pooling in comparison to the investment value. Liquidity can be achieved through adding other financial vehicles to a portfolio. Some experts such as Hegna and Olsen even venture to say that "Both agents and clients must stop applying investment mentality to risk transfer instruments." [11]

Further, more income, all else being equal, reduces the need for liquidity. Looking at two extremes: retiree A holds a portfolio consisting of 100% money market funds (very liquid) and retiree B holds a portfolio of 100% SPIAs (very illiquid). Retiree A will have no problem cutting a check to pay for a roof, so is in a good position from that standpoint if such an event were to occur. However, retiree A may have issues sustaining their entire retirement with minimal income. At the other extreme, retiree B may face issues absorbing the one-time expense. However, if its recurring income from the SPIA is high, he may be able to absorb the roof expense and cut down on other expenses for a short time frame.

This does not mean that liquidity is not important in retirement planning. It simply means that an increase in income can reduce the need for liquidity and that liquidity can be achieved through other products or asset classes.

Execution of Plan

Because SPIAs don't need to be managed and lack options, there is no requirement for monitoring. While the irreversibility nature of the SPIA can be thought of as a negative feature of the product, it can also be viewed positively as the simple nature and the lack of optionality can increase SPIA's desirability. Even for astute investor, this is an advantage as age may reduce this comfort or ability to manage personal finances. Further, SPIAs impose a good financial discipline.

IX.   Annuity Strategies and Mitigation

"An annuity should be viewed as a risk-reducing strategy, but it is instead often considered a gamble: "Will I live long enough for this to pay off?""

— Shlomo Benartzi, PhD
— Alessandro Previtero
— Richard H. Thaler, 2017 Nobel Prize Laureate in Economics
   2011 [7]

There are SPIA product features that mitigate early death risk such as cash refund and period certain. These can change the perceived value and the purchase decision process.

Period Certain

There is a well-understood fear that potential contract holders face when purchasing a life-only SPIAs: What if they die soon after signing the contract? The contract holder just wrote a significant check to the insurance company and will get little back. Even if the rationale makes sense, the emotional component associated with it is a major turn off. There are ways to overcome this issue. The inclusion of a period certain reduces this risk.

Using a numerical example, Table 1 contrasts IRRs for SPIAs with and without period certain. Both from a dollar amount and IRR perspective, an early death with a life-only annuity would be detrimental to Mike's estate. That's why period certain features exist in SPIAs; a period certain guarantees annuity benefit payments for a specific minimum period, such as 10 years. This guarantee comes at a cost, translated in reduced benefits. For example, a $6,127 life-only annuity benefit payment from a $100,000 SPIA life-only purchase, would be reduced to $6,000 to include a 10-year certain guarantee. If Mike dies at age 66 and a half, his benefit payment under the 10-year certain SPIA would look like:

- 2 payments of $6,000 paid to him while alive.
- 8 payments of $6,000 paid to estate after death.

This would result in a dollar loss of $40,000 ($100,000 – 10 x $6,000) and a negative (9.9%) IRR; not great but good downside protection and a scenario easier to accept than a negative (93.5%) IRR without a period certain.

Figure 4: IRR Based on Age at Death

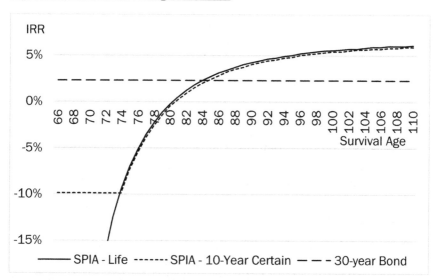

In case of an early death, IRR on a life-only SPIA is horrendous but there is a flip side to that coin. Looking at it another way, if Mike is willing to take that unlikely chance of early death, he will be rewarded by increased recurring benefit payments, in this case $127 annually. These dollars can be valuable 30 years from now, as many unknown factors — including personal, societal and economic environments — create uncertainty. These recurring dollars can be valuable as there is a cost associated with living. From an IRR perspective, if the annuitant is willing to take the risk of a significant large negative IRR in the event of an early death, he potentially gains from a slightly higher IRR in case of a later death.

Further, the question is, why would Mike leave a larger legacy if he dies early? If Mike can live on $6,000 income, he can elect that as a life-only benefit, pay a lower premium and leave the difference as a bequest.

The Denomination Factor

SPIAs are typically sold in large denominations making the purchase very emotional to investors. A $100,000 sale for most individuals is significant. Further, individuals buying a SPIA do not have something tangible to show for it, like a house. Even if the purchase is a rational thing to do, emotions get in the way of rationality, due to the large amounts of money involved. Laddering lifetime income in small tranches over time can help de-emotionalize the purchase.

In practice, SPIAs can be sold in large denominations, which makes such sale very emotional. The same expected results take a different dimension if they are carried at a lower level. For example, looking at the scenario where Mike passes away at age 66, hence receiving only two annuity payments of $6,127, the thought of losing $87,746 ($100,000 – 2 x $6,127) on a $100,000 investment when considering Mike and his estate as one entity is unthinkable for many. That's because for many individuals, $87,746 is a significant amount of wealth. It is 9% of a $1 million portfolio. However, losing $8,775 on a $10,000 investment may be a risk some may be willing to take because it is less than 1% of a $1 million portfolio.

While the loss from SPIA could be steep, the probability associated with this outcome is very low. Further, in this particular scenario, Mike would need less to fund his retirement, given he passed away earlier in this hypothetical scenario. The reverse could have been true, in which case he would have needed more funds to live, which the SPIA would have provided.

Several early-stage ventures have seen the day and address the need of creating a personal pension. [91] [92]

Buying Through Time

Fundamental financial concepts of risk reward and diversification apply to SPIAs, too. SPIAs bought on one particular day lock the annuitant into a benefit payment derived from pricing assumptions in a particular environment. In contrast, buying smaller amounts of SPIAs over time helps pre-retirees diversify over mortality, economic environments and credit exposure.

For example, a pre-retiree may be better off buying 20 SPIA contracts of $10,000 between the ages of 55 and 75-year-old, rather than a single $200,000 policy at age 65 for diversification purposes.

Getting Familiar with the Product

It may be appropriate for retirees and pre-retirees to spread their lifetime income purchases through time to allow them to gain familiarity with the product. As they understand benefits and drawbacks of the product, retirees can adjust their portfolio to their taste and calibrate that appetite over time.

Some individuals own properties which they partly occupy and partly rent. Duplexes in many cities where owners occupy the first floor and rent the top floor are popular across many countries. Entering in this type of investment involves many unknowns — for example, maintenance, ability to collect or raise rent. Getting in this type of arrangement for the first time at age 65 for example, as part of a retirement strategy can present fear. However, getting into this type of situation significantly before retirement allows retirees to understand the dynamics of such investment and could be in a better position to make the right decisions for themselves. The same holds for lifetime income; buying lifetime income products through time can help a pre-retiree understand the dynamic of the product and be more strategic with its SPIA purchases, as opposed to making few major decisions.

Medical Environment

A major medical breakthrough would increase the cost of SPIAs and timing such a discovery is nearly impossible. Purchasing smaller denominations through time, allows users expose themselves to various medical advancements environments, which have the possibility of impacting SPIA prices.

Economic Environment

SPIAs priced in a high interest rate environment result in higher annuity benefit payments and vice versa. Buying smaller amounts of SPIAs over time helps pre-retirees diversify over several economic environments.

Right Time

Buying SPIAs over a long period of time allows pre-retirees to fund their retirement at a time when they are usually in their prime earning period. It allows them to balance out current expenses and future retirement needs shaped to their always evolving situation. If or when a retiree's health deteriorates, he should avoid buying SPIAs, unless they are medically underwritten.

Wrapping up Annuities

There is a cost associated with living and if retirees are unable to meet their current expenses with investment income generated from their assets, they will be forced to sell those assets through time in the absence of lifetime income in their portfolio. The amount of assets desired to sell in order to meet current income requirements in any given retirement year will depend on asset prices at time of sale and remaining longevity estimates. If income need isn't flexible, selling assets may jeopardize bequest levels or, in an extreme case, cause longevity risk. On the flip side, using part of a retiree's portfolio to buy SPIAs or other forms of lifetime income can increase recurrent spending power due to mortality credits and allows retirees to exert a greater control on legacy. This course of action offers the benefits of increasing spending confidence and the ability to take advantage of investment opportunities with the remainder of the portfolio. [69] SPIAs are usually not the superstar offensive player of the team that reporters and fans adore but more the defensive player that doesn't necessarily make the headlines. However, SPIAs are the type of player that the coach who wants to win will pick first. The SPIA won't achieve spectacular results but it will allow other assets to be utilized to their full potential and eventually achieve the ultimate goal: building a sound retirement financial plan.

SPIAs have typically been portrayed as the very conservative investment favored only by risk-averse individuals. That's one point of view but the reality is that SPIAs can be quite risky: in the event of an early death, return on investment from the vehicle can be very low. At the same time, they can be quite rewarding because they allow investors to secure some lifetime income while at the same time pursuing more aggressive strategies with the rest of their portfolio. [69] Before purchasing a SPIA, individuals should understand the purpose, risks and mechanics of this specific financial vehicle to decide if it's a beneficial addition to a retirement investment portfolio. Considering such a purpose holistically, in light of an entire portfolio is important and should be analyzed the appropriate financial professionals.

Consider all the different liabilities you incur in your life such as a mortgage, utilities, car payments, cell phone plan. When you buy a SPIA, you put yourself in the opposite situation, transferring a liability from the insurance company to you.

Because time of death is unknown, lifetime income is an essential retirement planning tool. When considering the role of lifetime income, it is important to determine how the various elements of the retirement income puzzle, including yield, cash flows, tax and bequest amounts fit in on an integrated basis with the appropriate professionals.

X.   Tontines

"Tontines are a much-misunderstood investment arrangement that deserve a fresh look."

— Richard Fullmer, CFA
— Michael Sabin, PhD
  2018 [93]

Introduction

A tontine, in the current context, is a financial arrangement that individuals can enter whereby individuals pay an upfront sum of money in exchange for future payments, usually until death. Participants receive payouts while they are alive, which cease when they pass away. When they die, their stake in the arrangement is forfeited in favor of the remaining living participants of the fund. Tontines function much like annuities. However, technically they are not annuities because there is no party involved to assume risk. Tontines with different designs were used a few centuries ago and interest in the structure has resurfaced recently across the globe. [57] [59] [84] [93] [94] [95] [96]

History

Tontines originated in a proposal from Nicolas Bourey in Portugal, who proposed a tontine vehicle in 1641. Twelve years later, Lorenzo de Tonti proposed a tontine scheme, in 1653 in France. [94] Even if he was the second to propose such a structure, the word tontine derives from Tonti. Tontines were originally used by governments for raising funds from the population in the 17th century, sometimes for war purposes. [84] [94] [97] Various tontines were popular in Europe in the 17th century.

In his paper "A Short History of Tontines", McKeever provides an in-depth historical review of the different tontines that appeared over time, while discussing their legal aspects. He also effectively summarizes the important tontines that marked those centuries. In 1905, an industry embezzlement scandal led to the establishment of a New York state investigatory commission called the Armstrong Commission. At the time, New York state regulated the vast majority of the United States life insurance industry. Through the banning of what was known as deferred dividends, the Armstrong Commission effectively prohibited tontines in 1906. This occurred despite the fact that the problems surrounding tontines were due to related criminal activities rather than any specific issue related to tontines. [57] [97] Similar to McKeever, Ransom and Sutch bring historical insight to the topic, more specifically at the end of the 19th century when tontines were widely employed and how their improper activities brought tontines down. [98]

Embezzlement and fraud sadly continue to occur in modern society, but those types of activities related to investment funds haven't result in the banning mutual fund activities and rightfully so as millions of people benefit from mutual funds, which offer diversification and professional investment management to retail investors. Along the same lines, tontines, if structured appropriately, have the potential to offer lifetime income at a low cost and through various asset classes to retail investors. Ransom and Sutch argued that "tontines insurance was actuarially sound" meaning that "prohibition was probably unnecessary". [98] Further, Fullmer points out that society has evolved, creating many protection mechanisms that make it unlikely that the fraudulent activities that occurred in the early 20th century would happen again. [94] Also, McKeever points out that record keeping and plan administration have changed significantly since the time tontines were banned from the United States. [97]

Legality

Some countries, through private or public offering, have tontine-like product arrangements, including France and Sweden. [94] The U.K. allows tontines. [84] At the time this book is written, Canada and Australia demonstrate signs of a thaw in their previous rejection of tontines. [94] [99] Canada's recent potential regulation has paved the way for the possibility of tontine-like financial product offerings. [84] [94] [100] A community in South Africa has a tontine-like scheme in operation called Nobuntu, where funds are invested and redistributed in the future for funeral costs and long-term pensions. The regulatory environment in South Africa is generally loose and pooling financial resources within communities is not uncommon. [94] [99] [101] Japan insurance companies offer an insurance product called tontine pensions that includes tontine-like features. [99] The United States presents a trickier regulatory landscape due to its past history with tontines and the involvement of various state and federal authorities in the insurance and investment markets. New York state outlawed deferred dividends in 1906, which led to the disappearance on tontines in the country. South Carolina and Louisiana have statutes banning tontines. [97] In the US, Forman and Fullmer foresee regulatory hurdles for the implementation of TSAs; at the same time, the two experts have confidence that these obstacles can be surmounted. [102]

Types

Tontines were originally designed so that investment income was redistributed periodically to survivors, which meant that the last few surviving participants shared a hefty profit from the redistribution of the shares of the deceased participants. This design is known as the Lorenzo tontine. [103] This contrasts with a natural tontine as Milevsky, Salisbury, Gonzalez and Jankowski define as a tontine designed to provide relatively level continuous payments. [103] The natural tontine is also known as "constant-payout" or "level-payout" tontine. [84]

Models

Milevsky and Salisbury have formed a basis used in the public domain to describe and analyze tontines. [103] [104] [105] [106] [107] In recent years, a few papers have touched on how variations of the tontine concept could be adopted in the current environment. [97] A few examples of models and ideas are listed here. My review of this subject is not necessarily comprehensive. I apologize to other authors who have published on this topic whose work isn't discussed here.

One variation, described by Wadsworth et al. in "Reinventing Annuities" 2001, is the "annuitised fund". [108] In their 2005 paper, Piggott, Valdez and Detzel build a solid foundation for "group self-annuitization" and present a robust mathematical model. [109] Stamos builds on this model by discussing the optimization of consumption and asset allocation in the context of "pooled annuity funds". [110] Qiao and

Sherris analyzed multiple features of proposed models, including effectiveness of pooling at older ages. [111] In his 2007 paper "A Mutual Fund to Yield Annuity-Like Benefits," Goldsticker introduces a practical tontine mutual fund hybrid solution with a focus on practical applications and dynamics. [112] Baker and Siegelman propose a tontine concept in a non-longevity context: health coverage for young adults. [113] In his 2009 working paper, Rotemberg proposes a variation of tontines called a "Mutual Inheritance Fund" (MIF), where shares of deceased members are separated among surviving members, resulting in an increasing payoff between survivors through time. [114] His model differs from Goldsticker's by proposing increasing distributions, as opposed to annuity-like benefits. Sabin pioneered some tontine techniques and mathematical model; he then partnered with other experts to expand these ideas. [115] For example, in his 2010 paper, Sabin introduces yet another variation called the "Fair Tontine Annuity" (FTA), where he presents, among other things, a sophisticated algorithm to allocate deceased tontine members' shares back to surviving members. [86] Sabin partnered with Forman afterwards to model and offer practical thoughts to tontines. [116] Sabin partnered again, this time with Fullmer, to produce the paper Individual Tontine Account, offering a very practical application of what a modern tontine would look like. The piece even illustrates what an account statement would look like. [117] Tying it all together Milevsky, Salisbury, Gonzalez, Jankowski attached the Annuities vs. 21st century tontine in 2018. [103]

Need for Innovation

The idea of the need for innovation in the entire insurance space has been widely discussed. [45] More specifically, in the retirement income space, tontines adapted for the 21st century could be an innovative avenue for individuals if they can be brought to the markets.

XI.   <u>Survival Sharing</u>

"We need the iPad of retirement income."

— Moshe A. Milevsky, PhD
  2013 [118]

<u>Introduction</u>

The concept of Survival Sharing takes its inspiration from tontines. This financial vehicle is currently not available in the United States and many other jurisdictions. However, as mentioned in the prior chapter, just like tontines, possibilities and interest are looming in the horizon. Survival Sharing shifts the investment and the mortality risks to the group of investors in a way that aligns each individual with their expected spending while they are alive and protects them against longevity risk in a cost-efficient way. [30] Survival Sharing is a protection-oriented vehicle which shares similar characteristics with mutual funds, annuities, DB plans and tontines.

Survival Sharing consists of forming homogeneous closed groups of a sizable number of individuals possessing similar mortality characteristics, including age, gender, health condition, etc. Each participant contributes a specific amount to a fund. Participants forfeit their share of the fund to the benefit of surviving members. Similar to a traditional annuity, Survival Sharing consists of two phases: the accumulation phase and the distribution phase. The fund earns investment returns in the accumulation phase, in a manner analogous to a mutual fund. At a predetermined date, the arrangement shifts from the accumulation phase to the distribution phase, where the fund is redistributed periodically in an actuarially fair way to each surviving investor in small installments that are expected to last a lifetime, mimicking a DB pension plan payment. During each period, the remaining of the fund is shared among surviving members. The balance of the fund at each point in time depends on investment performance and the members' mortality. Assumptions to calculate the life annuity payments for the remaining members may also be recalibrated.

The structure consists of one master account that belongs to the surviving members. The balance of this master account before each payment is made depends investment returns and the mortality experience of the pool. Depending on that account value as well as expectations for future investment returns and mortality, distribution payments are calculated in order to calibrate the depletion of the master account with the intent to provide a fair recurring distribution payment for life to each surviving member.

A Survival Sharing arrangement does not guarantee future payments. The two assumptions in the distribution phase are investment performance and mortality. Fees also have to be embedded in the equation. Payments are calculated in a way that if the experience of the group in terms of mortality and investment returns is exactly as anticipated, the payments will be exactly as expected. In practice, this never happens. For example, for a group of 10 80-year-old men, the number of expected deaths over the next year is 0.58. In reality, zero, one or maybe two may die from the group, not 0.58. The same holds true for investment returns.

The Survival Sharing cycle differs from that of a traditional insurance product in that the latter is priced for and a premium paid for in exchange for future guaranteed benefit payments. In contrast, Survival Sharing pools individually identified investments of individuals before entering its iterative process of periodically redistributing the fund and adjusting payouts in an actuarially fair manner.

Each member receives a life annuity payment but since the group of investors is assuming the mortality and investment risk, the distribution amounts will vary over time.

Among other roles, the provider acts as an independent redistributor of the fund periodically. The goal of the provider is to keep payments close to the desired pattern predetermined in each pool, while simultaneously providing steady and reliable income to participants and protecting survivors against ruin.

Group size is relevant as a high number of participants is expected to decrease the annual fluctuation in income for each individual. Group homogeneity is of even greater importance in maintaining the overall fairness of concept. Individuals have the availability to reduce random variations by purchasing multiple pools of Survival Sharing through time. [30] [119] In this way the risk is diversified over several pools.

Differences

Survival Sharing differs from a DB pension plan or a life guaranteed product, which are vehicles that lock in a periodic payment. By guaranteeing a payment amount, one party has to assume the liability. In the case of a DB plan, the corporate sponsor guarantees life contingent payments to its employees at a certain point in time; this liability needs to be funded. Similarly, insurance companies guarantee life contingent payments or minimum withdrawal benefits for life to their contract holders; insurance companies establish a reserve and hold capital on the balance sheet in anticipation for this obligation. This guaranteed payment may sound comforting at first but, as discussed earlier, it comes at a cost.

In contrast, Survival Sharing does not lock in a fixed payment and does not incur any liability. Instead, it pools investments of homogeneous investors and redistributes the funds to survivors. Survival Sharing transfers the longevity risk to the pool of participants. Consequently, the cost from the provider's perspective is therefore significantly reduced and could potentially translates into savings for the consumer.

Features are virtually and anonymously settled between each member of a group, as opposed to incurring a charge or a penalty for a particular option or feature. As specific features become more popular, groups will form with those features, creating a supply and demand dynamic as opposed to a situation where pricing occurs based on specific features. If pools with a certain feature — such as those with high surrender charge — are sought out more than others, they will become more readily available. Investors who prefer other features may be forced to compromise on their preferences or on group sizes but these features will be shared among individuals and not priced as they are for insurance products. For example, a traditional FDA charging a high surrender charge should generate a higher crediting rate in comparison to another annuity charging a smaller surrender charge, all else being equal. With Survival Sharing, an individual can pick and choose their group and features, as long as personal characteristics align and other people want to be in the same group. The costs and options of each of those features are relative to the group and the individual can always be on both sides of the equation. For example, an individual can choose to be in a group with a 30% surrender charge in the accumulation phase. This means that if the individual withdraws their money from the fund during the accumulation period, he will only get 70% of the market value of their share and 30% will be distributed among the other members. This feature may be seen as a large penalty in case of withdrawal, but it also serves as a protection for the investor. The surrender charge discourages other members of the group from leaving the pool; individuals leaving the group decreases the number of lives pooled in the group, which could lead to larger income fluctuations during the payout phase. Further, the surrender charge provides for the ability to for the group to invest in longer term horizons. Perhaps most importantly, the surrender charge also serves as a potential benefit for the remaining investors, as the penalty incurred by the members leaving the group is distributed back into the fund. Unlike insurance products, the surrender charge is built into the relationship between the prospective members of a pool rather than between an individual and a financial institution. This introduces a dynamic where the provider is incentivized to offer groups the most popular features in order to get the right individuals together. (119)

Advantages

For Individuals

Allows Investing in Various Asset Classes

Survival Sharing offers the beneficial combination of mortality credits as well as investment in a wider range of asset classes. SPIAs currently provide lifetime income with an implied yield in line with the fixed income market. Survival Sharing allows individuals to buy lifetime income and reproduce the mortality credit mechanism, while investing in equities, real estate or other asset classes. Such an innovation would benefit customers, who are currently mostly limited to lifetime income with fixed income as an underlying return.

Provides Income
During retirement, generating income presents more challenges. Survival Sharing generates income at a time when individuals don't have a revenue they can count on anymore.

Effective for Managing Longevity Risk
Longevity risk requires a grouping mechanism such as pooling, hedging or insuring to function. Survival Sharing introduces an innovative method for individuals to manage longevity risk on their own through the use of pooling. Further, by using Survival Sharing, individuals are in a better position to control the desired legacy amount and create an estate that depends less on how long they will live. In this respect, they are similar to annuities.

Investment and Longevity Risk Are Not Related
SPIA and Survival Sharing are designed in the same way in the sense that the investor pays an outlay of funds upfront in return for periodical payments until death. SPIA and Survival Sharing differ in the sense that that SPIA payments are guaranteed by a third party, typically an insurance company, while Survival Sharing is facilitated by a third party that redistributes a fund and does not guarantee distribution payments. The mortality and investment return risks are assumed by the closed group of participants. This may be attractive as those two risks are unrelated. A major medical breakthrough or an economic downturn may happen but the two are not necessarily correlated.

Cost-Effective
Since Survival Sharing does not offer a guarantee, many costs associated with guarantees are saved and, consequently, passed back to the investor. [30] Sabin estimates "that insurers typically charge a premium that is 14% higher than fair." Sabin uses the word "fair" in a statistical way, where the 14% represents the difference between the full premium of what the insurer is charging for contract and the purely statistical position the insurer is assuming on the same contract. The 14% difference is essentially a load for profit and expenses, which is ultimately paid by contract holders. [86] Donnelly, Guillén and Nielsen reached the conclusion that participants in what they refer to as a "pooled annuity fund" could be keen to assume the mortality risk, under various scenarios. [120] Goldsticker also reached the conclusion that participants in such financial vehicle could see a financial advantage in assuming the mortality and investment risks. [112] McClelland reached similar conclusions. [92] Finally, Forman and

Fullmer point to a range of 10% to 15% of increased benefits with TSAs relative to life annuities. [102]

The expenses incurred by the Survival Sharing pool would most likely be lower than the expenses incurred for the income annuity.

A Survival Sharing provider incurs no liability for offering this product. Therefore, a Survival Sharing pool doesn't create large liabilities that need to be backed by general account assets on a corporate balance sheet because the provider doesn't assume risk.

Underwriting Burden on Participants' Shoulders

Traditional guaranteed income products are generally priced for healthy lives. Few carriers offer impaired annuities. Since longevity risk is a concern for all, Survival Sharing allows formation of groups of similar health, making it fair among participants.

In terms of underwriting, the procedure is the opposite of the underwriting process for life insurance. Life insurers need to assess the quality of health of a prospective policyholder in order to charge the appropriate price for the life insurance premium. The underwriting burden is on the life insurer's shoulders. In contrast, underwriting for lifetime income works the other way around. This means that participants are incentivized to disclose their health conditions because those disclosures facilitate appropriate pooling with a group of peers. Without such disclosure, unhealthy lives will be pooled with healthier ones, to the benefit of healthier lives. An administrator needs to validate the medical record in order to avoid falsified medical records but putting the underwriting burden on the participants and rewarding participants for disclosure eases the underwriting process.

Interest and technology geared towards efficient underwriting is in the process of development. This could eventually facilitate more efficient and effective underwriting processes for allowing underwriting for lifetime income products, including Survival Sharing.

Survival Sharing allows for customization for groups that share common characteristics. Individuals suffering from certain medical conditions may have lower life expectancies than others and see income annuities as an undesirable option. However, these individuals still face longevity risk. Survival Sharing allows people with similar medical conditions to form groups, generating an actuarially fair proposition.

Tailored and User-Defined Features

Survival Sharing enables a fair, dynamic and flexible feature-selection process. Each feature is ultimately shared equally among individuals so that each group member can participate on either side of the equation. Further, individuals can diversify over time on features, through subsequent purchase into other pools. They can also diversify on various mortality and economic environments.

Consistent Rules

Survival Sharing distribution payments may vary through time but the rules dictating those payments remain consistent, transparent and uniform through each contract. Because all major decisions in the Survival Sharing model are set when the participant enters a group, this serves to alleviate fear or lack of comfort regarding provisions.

Natural LTC And Medical Costs Hedge

In the United States, as individuals live longer, health care and LTC costs are likely to increase. Survival Sharing is not meant to be a substitute for LTC, health or disability insurance but does provide income at a critical time for certain individuals, in a similar fashion to SPIAs. Further, when it is too late for individuals to buy LTC because of impairment, medically underwritten lifetime income can be a useful tool to provide for LTC expenses. That's because the impairment results in higher Survival Sharing payouts, all else being equal.

No Provider Default Risk

Although insurer default with an annuity is not frequent, it is not out of the question. Survival Sharing eliminates default risk and relates income level to the asset exposure desired, as there are no contractual guarantees in the scheme.

Decision Making from a Position of Strength

Retirees often have to wrestle with tough decisions at a time when it is least convenient. In addition, as individuals age, there's an increasing risk of compromised judgment. For example, annuity contracts that include features for future election may end up confusing a retiree later in life. Survival Sharing enables more individuals to make informed decisions while they are still in a position of strength, confidence and security.

For Society

Provides a Financial Incentive to Stay Healthy

Survival Sharing incentivizes individuals to make healthy choices, since the longer they live, the more they will financially benefit from their investment.

Reduces Intergenerational Conflicts

With Survival Sharing, no segment of society is on the hook. Each group is self-sustainable and assets are redistributed by an independent party. Any deviation from the expected is reassessed each year. As a result, potentially contentious political issues are diffused.

Addresses Growing Concern of Longevity Risk

As a greater share of individuals are living in retirement and as lifespans increase, longevity risk will be a growing topic of interest and concern for a wide spectrum of organizations.

Increases Accessibility for Retirement Products

To date, various reasons including complexity have gone in the way of serving the middle market for many financial services products. Survival Sharing is designed to be accessible in a fashion that suits customers of the 21st century.

Reduces Need for Outside Regulation

Since many features of Survival Sharing are determined virtually among the pool members, the need for outside regulation is decreased. There's less need, for example, for mandated features such as surrender charges during the accumulation portion of the product that would not necessarily protect consumers. The Survival Sharing's group model empowers members of the pool to regulate themselves on many issues.

Other Applications

Survival Sharing in its pure structure applies to any individual seeking to reduce longevity risk and bequest risk. Variations of the concept exist and Survival Sharing can be structured in a different way and different contexts.

Baker and Siegelman suggested to apply the concept in a health care context, in this case for young adults. [113]

Survival Sharing arrangements could be applied to higher education; a pool could be formed among children where parents or grandparents contribute a certain amount to a fund growing at a certain rate of return. Redistributed funds can be used solely for college tuition. That way, funds from children who don't ultimately go to college due to a variety of factors subsidize the ones who do attend college. The living/death triggering event is switched to an attendance/no attendance at a higher education institution.

Conclusion

Survival Sharing brings together retirees and pre-retirees who share the same underwriting characteristics in a closed-end investment fund. Each participant agrees upfront to relinquish its stake upon passing away. Payments from the fund are set periodically to surviving participants; these distribution payments are recalibrated periodically based on the mortality experience of the group, investment returns as well as assumptions for future mortality rates and investment returns. This arrangement transfers the mortality and the investment risk to the closed group. It mirrors the payout of a SPIA but without the guarantee associated with it. The additional risk taking allows for diversification among more underlying asset classes and lower costs for participants. (30) (119)

The product is meant to be purchased in small multiple denominations over time; this allows participants to mitigate mortality and economic risks through various periods and cycles. In terms of economics, acquiring various tranches of Survival Sharing through time exposes individuals to various interest rate, stock market and real estate environments. That means that individuals can buy in at various times as medical science may change over time.

Its closed-end feature brings light to the actuarial black box [119]; while the calculations embedded within the arrangement are complex, they are traceable, fair and transparent. Further, the design of the product enables the bulk of the contractual agreements to be within individual participants, not between an individual and a corporation. The corporation acts as an independent redistributor and facilitates the arrangement rather than guaranteeing something. This creates a different dynamic, as the corporation provides only the pooling, administrative and investment functions; it charges a nominal fee for the service as opposed to guaranteeing a benefit which has to be priced for, as the participants share the mortality and investment risk.

In sum, Survival Sharing is a form of lifetime income in which participants give up their liquidity and principal when they pass away in exchange for mortality credits, as the product, just like a SPIA, requires an upfront payment from the participant in exchange for future periodical redistribution income payments for a lifetime. It turns assets into income, which is an important facet of retirement planning.

Survival Sharing is a cost-effective financial vehicle that allows participants to directly participate in a specific asset class while taking full advantage of the mortality credit dynamic without paying for the cost of the guarantee.

3. The Solution

XII.   Guiding Principles

*"It is a well-known fact that annuity contracts,
other than in the form of group insurance
through pension systems, are extremely rare.
Why this should be so is a subject of considerable
current interest. It is still ill-understood."*

— Franco Modigliani, 1985 Nobel Prize Laureate in Economics
1985 [121]

Guiding Principles

Understanding how the economic environment works and how each individual fit into the economic system is key to crafting a sound retirement plan.

There are a few fundamental guiding principles and recurring themes that shape the basis of the strategy for successful retirement income planning. These guiding principles serve as a reminder and steer retirees to build a successful strategy to support their retirement financial needs. Each decision should be assessed through the lenses of satisfying those guidelines.

Those guiding principles are:
- Funding a retirement for an unknown time span requires careful planning.
  - Time of death is unknown.
  - There is a variable cost associated with living.
- Retirees should be ready for a myriad of possible future paths that they may face.
  - Unknown time of death of an individual should not be guessed.
  - Future capital market returns should not be guessed.
  - Predicting future expenses should only be done when assessing if an individual is ready to retire and gauge expense level while in retirement.
- Bequest goals should be assessed and should not highly depend on time of death.
- Retirees, just like all other investors, should always be in a position of strength, not of need.
- Both income and assets are key and should periodically be assessed in tandem.
- Diversification in time of investment purchase, asset classes, product classes [81] and counterparties are important.
- Always add value to the portfolio.

Unknown Time Span

Time of Death Unknown

Time of death for most individuals is unknown. Instead of trying to predict the unknown the best way to mitigate longevity risk is appropriate planning based on analyzing both assets and income, regardless of the outcome of death. Time of death is a random variable with a probability distribution associated to it, just like the outcome from a roll of a die. There is probability of death associated with each future age, just like there is a probability that a given side of a die will be on the top after a toss.

Think about a regular fair die with six sides with numbers "1" to "6" labeled on the sides. Each side has a one out of six chances of occurring. If six people take a guess on the outcome of a die roll and each guess is different, one can assert with certainty that one person will guess the outcome right and five won't. Similarly, a person starting retirement has a probability of death during each year of the few upcoming decades. That outcome is unknown in advance.

In the retirement planning world, think of your age of death as a toss in the six-sided cube example. In this analogy, you only have one toss, you don't know what that outcome will be and the mean of the population surrounding you — your life expectancy — will provide minimal insight as to where you will land. Over a large group of reasonably healthy individuals, some will die earlier than others but each of those individuals has no visibility in advance what their outcome will be. While guessing at a casino can provide entertainment, guessing lifetime income needs can have dramatic consequences.

Life expectancy is often used as an important metric in retirement planning but it is merely a starting point of the discussion and should not be the focal point in decision making. Going back to the die example, if one tossed a die many times, recorded the outcome each time and computed the average of all outcomes, the results should be close to 3.5. The more die tossed, the more accurate that prediction should be. What does 3.5 mean for the outcome of the next die toss? Is the outcome going to be closer to "1" or "6"? The expected value provides no insight as to what the outcome of the next die toss will be.

There is a Cost Associated with Living

There is a variable cost associated with living. While alive, people eat, transport themselves, maintain residences, buy gifts for their grandkids, obtain services such as gardening or health care services and buy a myriad of items. In terms of retirement planning, it makes sense to plan accordingly. It therefore makes more sense to rely on more funds in the event of a longer life, at the expense of forgoing some of those funds in the event of a shorter. This can be achieved with lifetime income, as the mortality credit mechanism is a form of redistribution from people who die earlier than expected to others who die later than expected. From an income perspective, it is important that retirees can count on income for their entire lifetime, like when they were in their working years.

Assumptions Should not be Guessed

Insurance companies and other financial institutions often make future assumptions based on economic indicators or behavior of populations. This allows those firms to offer financial products and earn a profit over the long run. However, that same dynamic does not apply to individuals. Financial institutions perform those analyses with professional expertise on large groups of people using the law of large numbers. They further benefit from potential diversification among various lines of business. Finally, businesses are typically managed on an ongoing basis without necessarily a target end. This context is completely different than the environment that individuals live in. Here are the key assumptions that I believe retirees should not have to guess:

- Unknown time of death.
- Unknown future capital market returns.
- Future expenses are only estimates.

Unknown Time of Death

A non-terminally ill individual does not know their time of death. Life expectancy is a weighted average of a pool of individuals of the same age but it does not predict the time of death for specific individuals. Just like the average temperature for a given day in a year at a given place is not a precise prediction of what the temperature will be on that day at that place, life expectancy does not predict when a specific individual will die. A retiree turning 70-year-old today may suffer from a quick fatal accident a few days following his birthday but could also survive several decades. While those two scenarios are extreme, anything in between is also an unknown. The financial outcome in each case can also be extremely different if not managed properly.

Unknown Future Capital Market Returns

Predicting future capital market behavior is complex and risky. Many professionals dedicate their careers on taking various positions on the markets with significant resources that may not be available to individuals. This does not mean that retirees should not be opportunistic about how the markets behave. As always, professional guidance is recommended to navigate through various economic and capital market environments.

A strategy involving a systematic sell off of securities may not be optimal. That's because such behavior may not be advantageous to the investor. Golden argues that retirees should not bet their retirement savings on Monte-Carlo models. [39] Change in risk preferences combined with change in personal situations are all factors to be considered and one of the many reasons why working on an ongoing basis with a trusted advisor is important.

Future Expenses are only Estimates

While predicting future expenses is a useful exercise, determining what revenue will be used to cover those expenses is critical. This is true for both working years and retirement years. During working years, i.e. the accumulation phase, if an individual consistently spends more than he earns, financial difficulties are expected. This is true for the retirement years as well and perhaps even more so. That's because, since retirees mainly live on the income generated by their assets, overspending can result in the need to sell assets. Once those assets are sold, there is an inevitable reduction in future earning power. In addition, a need to quickly sell assets to finance spending may not be advantageous and can result in reduce future earning power.

Many pre-retirees aren't sure how to decide if they are ready to retire. One way to discern the answer is to compare existing expenses to the income that will be available in retirement. Establishing expenses first and working backwards can be a tricky exercise as retirees may run into issues if revenues are not enough to cover expenses. Further, expenses may vary dramatically through retirement, so the ability to adapt is important. For some, expenses may be higher in early retirement as people tend to be more active in those years. Conversely, especially in the United States, medical expenses, even with Medicare, may ramp up in later years of retirement. This is another good reason for retirees to generate a solid income base throughout retirement. A secure income base should translate to an enhanced ability to manage extra expenditures that may crop up during retirement.

Allowing expenses rather than income to drive the retirement bus can create issues. Alternatively, if income is generated and expenses occur within the income boundaries, the retiree can have more confidence in his spending power and recalibrate his asset and income portfolio from a position of strength, not of need.

Bequest Goals Should be Assessed

Retirees counting on periodically selling assets and not utilizing lifetime income through their retirement to provide for themselves will most likely leave a significant bequest to their heirs if they pass away early. Conversely, they will most likely leave a low inheritance to their heirs if they live much longer than expected, all else being equal. In a more extreme case, if they pass away significantly later than expected, they may leave negative legacy in the sense that family or a social mechanism may be required to take care of them. Negative bequest can be viewed as longevity risk.

Always Be in a Position of Strength, not of Need

Capital markets are complex, which means that stock and bond prices can fluctuate widely. Counting on selling assets in the future to cover expenses can result in sub-optimal outcomes. Potentially the worst outcome for retirees is a situation in which unfavorable markets occur at the beginning of retirement, leading to asset depletion affecting all subsequent years. This is known as sequence of return risk, a factor that increases longevity risk.

Alternatively, if that same individual can count on stock dividends, bond coupons and lifetime income to provide ongoing income, there may be less of a need to sell stocks during a potentially unfavorable market environment. A retiree may change preferences through time for taking more or less risk by changing investment allocation and strategy. As long as assets remain, future potential earning power remains, all else being equal. Buying lifetime income is also an option. The key is to do balance a portfolio of assets and income from a position of strength, not of need. With sufficient ongoing income, retirees can place themselves in a position where they aren't forced to sell assets at a given time.

Income and Assets in Tandem

In the broad function of financial analysis — including but not limited to credit or equity — a myriad of studies, regulations and statements are analyzed. However, in one way or the other, this information ends up in two fundamental statements: the balance sheet and the income statement. Ignoring one or the other involves missing a significant part of the story as the two statements convey different information and feed each other.

Personal finance is no exception to that. A personal balance sheet can be easily constructed by adding all of an individual's account value statements from bank accounts, brokerage accounts, mutual fund holdings or other asset holdings and fair value of lifetime income. On the income statement side, an income statement can be created by adding all income generated from assets and lifetime income.

During the working years, the accumulation phase, revenues are typically salaries, bonuses, commissions or other forms of compensation realized as a result of work performed. During retirement, the decumulation phase, revenues are typically generated from assets accumulated during working years. The balance sheet continues to be easy to track down with account value of various holdings. However, the generation of the income statement is more nebulous. It can be a challenge for individuals to generate and manage income so as not to overspend or under-spend. Underspending doesn't create as much of a risk as overspending but the risk still exists. If retirees spend too little, they risk failing to take full advantage of the benefits of retirement. Striking that right balance with an unknown period to spend the funds is where guaranteed or planned lifetime income can help.

Knowing how much the value of a retiree's assets are worth is important; equally important is how much those assets can generate income without running out of money. The former is readily available, the latter is more of a challenge.

Diversification

Buying lifetime income periodically through time can be beneficial as it provides diversification. For example, in a high interest environment, SPIA benefits tend to be higher, all else being equal. Also, in a hypothetical period following a major scientific medical discovery, SPIA benefits could decrease, as the income provider expects to pay benefits for a longer period of time. Again, individuals should not guess future medical breakthroughs or interest rate environments, so buying various SPIAs over time offers the advantage of diversification across uncontrollable events.

Diversification among asset classes has been discussed at length in financial literature. Gaining access to various options and sources can be beneficial for retirees.

Credit risk on bonds and SPIA providers, is a key risk. Relying on outside credit quality ratings can help mitigate this risk. Insolvency can create discontinuity in payments. Diversification among various carries as well as relying on credit ratings can be risk strategies for retirees.

Always Add Value to Portfolio

Retirees should always construct their portfolio in a way that adds value. Adding lifetime income can be an important value-creating consideration but only if it's actuarially fair. For example, a person with impaired health should not buy lifetime income unless the lifetime income vehicle is underwritten to recognize the impaired health.

<u>Wrapping up Guiding Principles</u>

It is important to keep in mind those founding principles as they will form a guiding basis for the AIM. While financial institutions offer financial guarantees, make assumptions about the future, price and manage the products on a higher scale, this dynamic does not necessarily apply to individual retirees. Because of the risk pooling capabilities financial institutions have, individuals can benefit from such guarantees.

Further, avoiding assumptions prevents a false sense of confidence regarding future events. For example, is assuming equity returns slightly less than historical averages really a conservative assumption? Or does assuming one will live a few years longer than their life expectancy mean that longevity risk is off the table? The answer is hopefully no; however, there is really no way to know, so prudent and diversified planning can help individuals avoid a false sense of confidence.

Finally, whether a retirement plan succeeds or fails over the long term may hinge on small margins or subtle decisions. Making the decision of retiring or waiting an extra year or two can have a significant impact on retirement. AIM, which I will explain in the next chapter, provides a framework that will allow individuals to deal with their individual situation in an appropriate way.

XIII.   The Asset to Income Method

"The addition of annuity payments to the dividends and interest your portfolio generates guarantees income for life and smooths out the volatility that hangs like a dark cloud over other plans. That makes your planning much simpler, because you no longer must be totally dependent on the stock and bond markets."

— Jerry Golden, MAAA
2019 [39]

Introduction

The Asset to Income Method (AIM) tackles retirement financial planning in a strategic way through fundamental principles. The framework addresses all issues in section 1 and utilizes lifetime income, discussed in section 2, as a central piece of the approach.

AIM consists of creating a structured financial mindset that is based on fundamental investment and risk pooling principles. Individuals who employ AIM can construct a financial plan they can count on throughout their retirement. This framework will take into account major future unknowns such as life span and investment returns.

Looking back at the basic principles, income and asset value should be considered in tandem; investors should always be in control. The key feature of this approach is the tradeoff between expected bequest and recurring income during retirement. Further, lifetime income is the financial vehicle that provides retirees with the flexibility to strike the right balance between the two. As part of this dynamic process, retirees will experience changes in income and expected legacy as well as variance in asset classes, risk appetite, liquidity needs or personal situations. All these factors must be constantly reassessed from a position of preference and strength, not of need. Individuals may require the assistance of financial professionals to navigate through specific products, markets or tax environments. While pure lifetime income is currently available in limited varieties, new ideas are likely to emerge in the future. (59)

AIM

The AIM approach solution consists of assessing:
A. Total value of traditional assets.
B. Total income generated from assets in A.
C. Lifetime income.
D. Permanent life insurance.
E. A buffer fund representing a small portion of the total portfolio for liquidity, emergencies and flexibility.

Use the assessments above in the following way:

1. Use A + D as an estimation for bequest.
2. Use B + C as an estimation for recurring income available to spend.
3. Calibrate 1 and 2 with lifetime income:
    a. If income (step 2) is too low and bequest (step 1) can be sacrificed, increase lifetime income.
    b. If bequest (step 1) is too low and income (step 2) can be sacrificed, reduce lifetime income.
4. Use E as an emergency fund for liquidity and unforeseen events and as a general cushion.

In other frameworks, Golden defines B as "Recurring income from savings / investments" and C as "Guaranteed and lifetime income". (122) Shemtob defines E as the "Emergency fund". (123)

Detailed Assessment

Use the assessments above in the following way:

1.   Use A + D as an estimate for bequest.

The market value of total assets, including both invested assets and life insurance, can be used as an order of magnitude for a potential bequest. It is one of many views a retiree should consider. The dollar value amount provides an order of relative magnitude. Inheritance goals can be measured in different ways other than dollar value. Shares, units, stake in an investment, jewelry and property provide a lens. Stock prices vary every minute but a number of shares of a specific stock or fund, while far from a guarantee, can provide some relative value over time. Similarly, real estate may or may not provide rental property income and its future market value is unknown but leaving the property to heirs, regardless of the market value of the property on the day it is left as a legacy, does provide some relative consistency over time. [37] It is also important to note that there may be sentimental value associated with certain assets, such as a historical family house or jewelry, which should also be taken into consideration. Securities such as stocks and bonds should not fall in this category.

The asset allocation and specific securities should be analyzed by a professional financial advisor in order to assess a myriad of considerations including but not limited to personal situation, capital markets and taxes.

2.   Use B + C as an estimate for income available to spend.

Income generated is ongoing income retirees can count on, just like the salary they earned while working. B includes dividends on stocks and coupons on bonds, while C includes SPIAs, a pension from a DB plan or a public old-age pension program. Just like assets in "1", this estimation is meant to be a check on the order of magnitude one can expect in recurring income. Risk and reward in various future economic and personal situation need to be assessed, hence the need to work with a financial professional.

3.   Calibrate 1 and 2 with lifetime income.

If income is too low and bequest can be sacrificed, one option is to buy lifetime income, assuming it is an appropriate purchase based on a health assessment. Examples include SPIAs, DIAs, VAs or FIAs with guaranteed minimum withdrawal benefits but other products may emerge in the future, including Variable Income Annuities (VIAs), Survival Sharing or tontines. Another way to generate additional lifetime income is to optimize public old-age pension program lifetime income benefits. For example, in the United States, delaying the election of Social Security can be an effective way to boost lifetime income as long as an individual is healthy and can afford to do so. [66]

If bequest is too low and income can be sacrificed, one option is to reduce the amount of lifetime income. In practice, options may be limited but cashing in a DB pension for a lump sum can be an example of that. Before taking this action, investors should consider many factors with a professional advisor. Another way to achieve a goal of leaving a larger bequest is to avoid spending all the proceeds from lifetime income. While lifetime income is designed to be spent, there is no requirement that it must be spent. By reinvesting lifetime income proceeds, a retiree could increase the future bequest.

4.   Liquidity.

Establishing a buffer fund representing a small portion of total assets — 5% - 10% of assets depending on circumstances — can provide retirees with the flexibility to pivot appropriately if unforeseen events occur. For example, LTC expenses in the United States or property maintenance if retiree owns property are good examples of that. That fund needs to be fully invested — no income withdrawal — in diversified and accessible assets to serve as a safety net for unexpected expenses. The amount allocated to this fund could be decreased under certain circumstances, including the presence of LTC insurance coverage. The funds can also fill the gap on a financial loss that is not expected to recur, for example, a credit loss. Such an emergency fund is not designed to specifically take care of all unforeseen events; but instead provide retirees with an extra lever to pull to rebalance appropriately. Further, this buffer or emergency fund should be replenished if it is deployed for other purposes such as rebalancing.

5.   Life Insurance.

Life insurance can be used in many ways. Its first intent is to protect a younger breadwinner' family facing significant future expenses in the event of the breadwinner's death. It is meant to protect the human capital of such breadwinner. [81] Life insurance can also have a longer horizon and contribute to legacy goals. If retirees possess life insurance and plan on continuing it, this asset should be factored into the retirement income equation.

Comments on the Process

This whole process remains dynamic so that at each point in time, finances, personal situations, risk appetite and goals can be reassessed. Life insurance should be assessed through this process using the fundamental principles. Options, such as keeping the policy in force to leave the face amount as a bequest or lapsing and reinvesting what would have been future premiums are alternatives that need to be analyzed with a professional agent. Health status is a top consideration when it comes to analyzing life insurance management. As always, advice from an agent, advisor or other professionals is often beneficial.

Details

Some of the major advantages of employing AIM include control, ease of execution, ability to manage unknowns, avoiding negative consequences of longevity risk and shifting the traditional dilemma of "spending rate vs. probability of ruin" to "spending rate vs. expected bequest".

Being in Control

The AIM allows investors/retirees to remain in a position of strength, not of necessity. Selling securities or assets is an option, not a requirement. Depressed asset prices and unfavorable sequence of returns are unwanted surprises to retirees. AIM also allows investors, if desired, to retain an opportunistic investment posture.

Potential opportunistic scenarios include:

- A retiree a few years into retirement with an increasing appetite for recurring secure income could decide to change asset or income allocation. This shift could allow that individual to lock in gains and secure a more predictable income stream.
- A handy retiree in good health who wants to deploy time and capital could decide to buy property. In the short term, that retiree can invest time and money in the property. In the long term, after making some improvements, that retiree can decide whether to sell, rent or occupy that property, depending on circumstances at that time.

Needs and uses of lifetime income may change over a retirement. For example, a retiree may decide to purchase more lifetime income after several years in retirement. While it is not designed for this purpose, if a retiree has sufficient income and wants to increase the expected legacy, that retiree can reinvest some or all of the lifetime income. Individuals in poor health should avoid purchasing lifetime income unless it is fairly underwritten.

Unknown Time of Death

The AIM allows retirees to have the confidence in spending, despite their unknown date of death. The ability to evaluate expected value of assets and income provides a valuable sense of control over retirement management. Assets are income generators; if retirees keep assets through their retirement, they may retain their earning power. If they periodically sell those assets to provide for themselves, they decrease their earning power. If retirees knew in advance how long they would live, this would not be a problem, as needed cash flows could be easily planned. But since this is not the case, retirees need to exert some level of conservatism with their drawdown approach. If a retiree does not maintain a conservative approach with their assets, they run the risk of depleting assets before they die, which is longevity risk. Conversely, not consuming funds fast enough can lead to unnecessary decrease in standard of living due to fear of longevity risk. This can also mean forgoing possible medical treatment. Lifetime income helps optimally generate income.

Execution is Realistic
The AIM works well for all types of retirees, including savvy investors who trade securities frequently or passive investors. Retirees can automate a consistent stream of income through scheduled transfers of investment income generated from a brokerage account into a checking account. This can bring extra comfort to retirees, knowing that the strategy can be executed by someone else in the event of incapacitation.

Bequest
Expected legacy should not solely depend on time of death and should not be measured solely in dollars. While no one knows the value of real estate, private equity, fixed income assets and equity markets through time, a bequest of property X, face value of a bond of $Y and 100 shares of stock Z does have some constant relative value in time. Also, an inheritance goal may be 0, in which case lifetime income helps retirees realize their full income potential. [5] Not assessing an inheritance goal may create a missed opportunity on the income side of the equation. [37] Not achieving bequest goals can be disappointing on the one hand but can also be a source of unnecessary curbed spending while alive. Both outcomes are not desirable and can be avoided with the use of the AIM. AIM allows retirees to formulate a desired balance between income and legacy is that not predominantly depending on longevity.

Avoid Longevity Risk
The risk of running out of funds to live on can be a significant risk, known as longevity risk. Employing the AIM results in natural alarms significantly before this outcome, helping retirees ask themselves the right questions through retirement.

Health-related Expenses

This part is addressed to individuals living in nations where health care costs are mostly borne by individuals. The United States is a good example of that, as it has a private health care system and the cost of health care is high, although Medicare mitigates some of that risk. Cost sharing under Medicare is another unknown retirees face. An individual does not know in advance if he/she will die from a sudden death or a slowly degenerating disease or how much the health care associated with treating those health situations will cost.

Just like other expenses, there is a variable cost associated with health care expenses, including routine check-ups or procedures occurring at a higher frequency at higher ages. Stated otherwise, a retiree is most likely going to incur more health care expenses if he/she were to live a very long life, all else being equal.

There is also an unknown part of health care costs that relates to the type of disease an individual suffers from. This is one example of where the buffer fund can be handy. For example, dementia related diseases can be particularly expensive, as retirees suffering from those conditions require significant caregiving assistance. Further, insurance products, such as LTC insurance help with those issues, as it pools this risk among a population where some may conduct the illness and others may not. Depending on insurance coverage, the needed emergency fund size may change.

The emergency fund may be seen as a small allocation to liquidity. This size of allocation — 5 to 10% — may not cover all needs that arise, especially in terms of LTC expenses. The AIM is designed to achieve an optimal balance between assets and income, such that the portfolio generates income in an optimal way. The buffer is meant to provide financial flexibility, should a financial plan need to shift.

Contrasts with Other Strategies

The AIM allows retirees to plan for their retirement while contending with the unknown length of their lifetime spans. Any drawdown approach calls for selling assets in the future to provide for one's needs. There are various issues with this, including sequence of return risk.

Also, retirees are faced with a tradeoff between drawdown amount and probability of running out of funds. The AIM addresses these issues and shifts the tradeoff from drawdown and probability of ruin to a tradeoff of income while alive and bequest.

Alternatively, bond laddering approaches can be used to tackle the need to sell assets at specified times. However, this does not address legacy and longevity issues in tandem, whether too high or too low, as a bond laddering approach requires picking a lifetime span upfront. If the retiree does not pass away around that targeted time, the strategy will either create longevity risk or inadequate inheritance if the time picked is too soon. In contrast, if the time picked is too long, an unnecessarily lack of spending and the potential for unnecessarily high inheritance could occur. The AIM also avoids this guessing of time of death by offering a solution with a revenue stream for a lifetime and a bequest that is less dependent of time of death.

Wrapping up AIM

The AIM allows retirees to have full confidence throughout retirement, while exerting a greater bequest control, regardless of how long they live. It follows the founding principles that were laid out earlier that are essential to tackle the financial challenges of retirement.

The AIM is a model that allows retirees to plan for their retirement. There is a famous saying from Box in statistics: "Essentially all models are wrong but some are useful." [124] Everyone's personal situation is different and each individual's situation changes over time. The AIM is not meant to be rigid; its purpose is to highlight the dynamics involved in the multitude of risks retirees face, which include asset value, income, unknown time of death, inheritance etc. For this reason, the plan needs to be reassessed regularly. The AIM is a framework and an invitation to the reader to think about assets, insurance and lifetime income. It is not advice or recommendation to purchase, hold or sell any type of security or insurance product. In practice, professional advice is recommended to assess personal situation, market conditions, tax implications and many other types of advice professional advisors perform.

XIV.   Practical Example

"Our favorite holding period is forever."

— Warren E. Buffett
  1989 [125]

Case Scenario

This chapter will present hypothetical, illustrative and practical examples that will evaluate the tradeoff of lifetime income and bequest through the AIM.

Case 1

Table 11 summarizes Case 1, a typical portfolio with a fair value of $1 million, including all financial vehicles. The portfolio consists of traditional asset classes such as fixed income, equities and real estate. It also includes the retiree's main home as well as lifetime income: a small DB plan and Social Security. It does not include a SPIA. Finally, it has a small emergency fund. Case 2 will illustrate the impact of the purchase of lifetime income on each component.

Table 11: Case 1, Base Scenario

Case 1: Typical Retiree Portfolio Allocation

Category	Allocation
Traditional invested assets	30.0%
Real Estate	35.0%
Lifetime income	32.5%
Emergency fund	2.5%
Total	100.0%

Case 1: Detailed Financial Vehicles

Category	Subcategory	Fair Value	Payout Rate	Periodic Amount
Traditional Assets	Fixed income	150,000	3.0%	4,500
	Equities	150,000	2.0%	3,000
Real Estate	Investment	100,000	5.0%	5,000
	Residence	250,000	0.0%	0
Lifetime Income	Public	300,000	7.0%	21,000
	DB plan	25,000	7.0%	1,750
	SPIA	0	7.0%	0
Emergency	Miscellaneous	25,000	0.0%	0
Total		1,000,000		35,250

Case 1: Results

Value	Amount
Fair value of the portfolio	1,000,000
Ongoing Income	35,250
Expected Bequest	650,000

Fixed Income

This example will assume that the portfolio of bonds is worth $150,000 and yields 3%. This may be invested in the form of the aggregation of a few bonds or it can be held within a fund. Regardless, the plan should involve retaining the bonds until maturity while periodically spending the coupons. Selling or buying bonds could be done opportunistically, depending on change in need or appetite but such potential sell is not designed to cover living expenses. Further, as these securities mature, individuals can reassess their appetite for each specific class. That way, retirees can leave the face amount as a bequest and the coupons generated from these securities can be used as ongoing income.

Specifications:
- Fair value $150,000
- Payout rate   3.0%
- Ongoing income estimate $4,500
- Current bequest estimate $150,000

Equities

This example will assume that the portfolio of stocks is worth $150,000 and the dividend yields is 2%. This may be invested in the form of the aggregation of a few stocks or it can be held within a fund. Regardless, the plan should be to hold on to shares forever and periodically spend the dividend. Selling or buying stocks could occur opportunistically, depending on changes in need, appetite or market conditions. However, buying and selling is not designed to occur to fund expenses. That way, retirees can leave shares as a bequest and the market value of these shares can be used as a current estimate for such an inheritance. While not a guarantee, the current market value of assets can serve as an order of magnitude of bequest and income. Both value of assets and income can fluctuate over time.

Specifications:
- Fair value $150,000
- Payout rate   2.0%
- Ongoing income estimate $3,000
- Current bequest estimate $150,000

Real Estate

This example assumes that the portfolio of real estate is worth $100,000 and yields 5%. This may be invested in the form of the aggregation of shares in a real estate fund or direct ownership of a portion of a building held as an investment generating revenues. Regardless, the plan should be to hold on to the property and periodically spend the investment income. Selling or buying ownership in the property may be done opportunistically and depending on change in need or appetite but not to provide for expenses. That way, retirees can leave the property as a bequest and the market value of these properties can be used as a current estimate for such an inheritance. While not a guarantee, the current market value of properties can serve as an order of magnitude of bequest and income.

The income generated from this real estate investment can be used as revenue. This example could apply for various other investments, including family or side businesses.

Specifications (Real estate invested assets):
- Fair value $100,000
- Payout rate   5.0%
- Ongoing income estimate $5,000
- Current bequest estimate $100,000

As for a retiree's home, assuming the mortgage is paid off, the assumption is that no revenues are generated from the main residence, although some do rent their main residence from time to time. It is further assumed that the residence will be left as a bequest.

Specifications (Real estate main residence):
- Fair value $250,000
- Payout rate   0.0%
- Ongoing income estimate $0
- Current bequest estimate $250,000

Public Old-Age Pension Program

This example assumes that the public old-age pension program pays $1,750 per month, hence $21,000 per year. Using the proxy income annuity payout of 7%, the estimated the value of this benefit is $300,000. It is important to note that the $300,000 fair value is an estimation of the value of the benefit; it is not a market value or a cash value as these benefits are usually not tradable. This benefit ceases when the retiree passes away and the income generated from this benefit is ongoing income.

Specifications:
- Fair value $300,000
- Payout rate   7.0%
- Ongoing income estimate $21,000
- Current bequest estimate $0

Private Pension

This example assumes that a private pension pays $145.83 per month, hence $1,750 per year. Using the proxy income annuity payout of 7%, the estimated the value of this benefit is $25,000. This benefit is assumed to cease when the retiree passes away — unless there is a spousal survivorship benefits — and the income generated from this benefit is ongoing.

Specifications:
- Fair value $25,000
- Payout rate   7.0%
- Ongoing income estimate $1,750
- Current bequest estimate $0

Aggregation of Case 1
Going back to the initial method:

A. Total value of invested assets $650,000
B. Total income generated from A $12,500
C. Lifetime income $22,750
D. Permanent life insurance $0
E. Keeping a buffer fund for liquidity $25,000

Use assessments above in the following way:

1. Use A + D as estimate for bequest $650,000
2. Use B + C as estimate for income $35,250
3. Calibrate 1 and 2 with lifetime income:
   a. If income is too low and bequest can be sacrificed, buy lifetime income.
   b. If bequest is too low and income can be sacrificed, reduce lifetime income.
4. Use E as a buffer fund for liquidity $25,000

Case 2
Going back to step 3a, assuming the retiree is healthy, the question becomes: is the combination of an estimated bequest of $650,000 and recurring yearly income of $35,250 a good combination? Let's assume the answer is no as income is too low and bequest can be sacrificed. The course of action could be to increase lifetime income. In this illustrative example, we will look at the impact of decreasing assets by $100,000 (decrease equities by $50,000 and decrease fixed income by $50,000) towards the purchase of a $100,000 SPIA. Here is the impact of these transactions:

Fixed Income: Expected bequest decreases by:
$50,000
Expected recurring incomes increase by:
(7% - 3%) * $50,000 = $2,000

Equity: Expected bequest decreases by:
$50,000
Expected recurring incomes increase by:
(7% - 2%) * $50,000 = $2,500

Total: Expected bequest decreases by:
$50,000 + $50,000 = $100,000
Expected recurring incomes increase by:
$2,000 + $2,500 = $4,500

The new approximation assessments of the portfolio are the following:
1. Estimated bequest, A + D: $550,000
2. Estimated Ongoing income, B + C: $39,750

Aggregation of Case 2

Case 2 shows the tradeoff between income and bequest with lifetime income serving as a calibrator. Table 12 summarizes the numbers.

Table 12: Case 2, Convert Some Invested Assets to SPIA

Case 2: Typical Retiree Portfolio Allocation

Category	Allocation
Traditional invested assets	20.0%
Real Estate	35.0%
Lifetime income	42.5%
Emergency fund	2.5%
Total	100.0%

Case 2: Detailed Financial Vehicles

Category	Subcategory	Fair Value	Payout Rate	Periodic Amount
Traditional Assets	Fixed income	100,000	3.0%	3,000
	Equities	100,000	2.0%	2,000
Real Estate	Investment	100,000	5.0%	5,000
	Residence	250,000	0.0%	0
Lifetime Income	Public	300,000	7.0%	21,000
	DB plan	25,000	7.0%	1,750
	SPIA	100,000	7.0%	7,000
Emergency	Miscellaneous	25,000	0.0%	0
Total		1,000,000		39,750

Case 2: Results

Value	Amount
Fair value of the portfolio	1,000,000
Ongoing Income	39,750
Expected Bequest	550,000

These simple examples illustrate the mechanics of how lifetime income increases recurring income and decreases legacy over a full portfolio, using the AIM. These examples are not meant to encompass specific nuances of every asset class; fair value, payout rate, ongoing income estimate and current bequest estimate are subject to change continuously and constantly need to be recalibrated frequently, based on personal situation, market conditions and risk appetite to name a few variables.

Striking the right balance between the income and bequest is a question of preference and need. Lifetime income is the vehicle that helps achieve this balance. Again, the AIM is not meant to be rigid and a guarantee of bequest and recurring income; rather it gives an order of magnitude and a framework for retirees to navigate and recalibrate needs and goals over time from a position of strength. These illustrative examples broaden the discussion, but individuals should discuss and assess their specific situations with one or more financial professionals in order to evaluate actual asset classes, benefit values, tax implications and personal situations on an ongoing basis.

XV.   Other Risks and Contrarian Thinking

"Longevity risk is actually a risk multiplier:
the longer you live, the more exposed
you are to all the other risks."

— Tom Hegna, CLU, ChFC, CASL
2011 [20]

How Other Risks Fit in

Other Risks Retirees Face

While the focus of this book is on longevity risk, retirees face a myriad of other risks. Addressing those risks through the lens of AIM provides a powerful perspective. In general, just like any other financial framework, diversification is a key common denominator in reducing risks. The Lifetime Income Risk Joint Task Force — now a Committee — of the AAA identifies the following lifetime income risks: [126]

- Longevity risk
- Long-Term Care (LTC) costs
- Health care costs
- Inflation
- Investment performance and volatility

Starting with those risks as a solid foundation, ignoring longevity risk because it is the dominant topic of this book, other risks during retirement have been identified:

- Sequence of return
- Liquidity
- Fraud
- Cognitive impairment
- Credit and default
- Taxation

Now we will go through each risk in more detail, revealing strategies for containing them through the lens of AIM.

LTC Costs

LTC costs in the United States can come with a hefty price tag. In addition, whether and when they will be incurred are unknowns. For this reason, LTC insurance mitigates this risk. [127] Some retirees may be in a financial position to self-fund long-term care through the buffer fund or large amounts of ongoing income. Underwritten SPIAs, which provide a larger income in recognition of poor health, can also be an avenue that turns cash into attractive lifetime income if LTC insurance isn't an option.

AIM is designed as a flexible system that doesn't foreclose the possibility of selling assets to provide for LTC costs. That being said, once those assets are liquidated and spent, they aren't available as an income stream or a bequest. Because it's important for retirees to operate from a position of strength, a diversified portfolio provides choices in how to fund LTC expenses.

The AIM generates and clearly identifies a revenue stream. The risk of LTC involves the risk of incurring hefty expenses for care. Under the AIM lenses, the risk is the difference between the recurring cost of care and the current revenue stream. The higher the revenue stream is, the lower the risk.

To attach numbers to this situation, consider a $1 million portfolio, generating 5% income — a weighted average of 2% dividends yield, 3% bond coupons and 7% SPIAs and Social Security — on $900,000 which equates to $45,000 per year with a buffer fund of $100,000. One way to use this emergency fund for LTC expenses involves splitting it over two years, allocating $50,000 each year. The result? A total of $100,000 for LTC expenses over those two years, which might not be enough. However, coupled with current recurring income, it provides $95,000 per year for two years that can go towards LTC expenses, which is a good start. In the above example, assuming this person has no LTC insurance, the AIM buys some time to come up with a longer-term solution. Selling assets at the cost of bequest can be an option and this is where time and flexibility can be key. Using an emergency fund as a buffer allows retirees to strategize how they manage the depletion of assets from a position of strength. As soon as there is a need for LTC funds, retirees can also explore the possibility of underwritten SPIAs as they are an available tool to cope with this situation. (83) Reverse mortgage can also be an option to cope with LTC costs. All these options and dilemmas should be explored with the appropriate experts in any given jurisdiction.

Health Care Costs
Health care costs in the United States can be high in retirement, although some of those costs are covered by Medicare. It is important to note that health care costs may be irregular and tend to rise substantially near end of life. That being said, a significant amount of health care costs tends to vary with life span, including routine doctor visits, medication or other treatment of chronic conditions that develop over time.

The average cost of health care for an American retired couple — not including long-term care — is estimated at $295,000. (128) Analogous to life expectancy, this number is an average, not a figure specific to any single situation. Accumulating this amount and setting it aside is the beginning rather than the end of the exercise. There are fixed and variable components embedded within this amount. Most importantly, exactly what those costs will be and when they occur is unknown in advance. The AIM accounts for this situation, facilitating a retiree's ability to successfully navigate through this dynamic.

Inflation
Inflation is a major concern in retirement because it exerts an unknown impact on a retiree's purchasing power. Even if a retiree's investment portfolio performed as expected, the real value of those returns can significantly decrease due to inflation. Inflation represents a major concern for young retirees as they potentially face decades of unknown economic environments. Further, inflation affects various people in different ways. (81) For example, medical inflation may outpaced general inflation benchmarks in a certain jurisdiction. The implication of this trend means that a retiree facing high medical costs will be impacted more by inflation than a healthier person. The Consumer Price Index (CPI) is a measure of inflation. Milevsky argues that this

metric does not impact everyone equally. In fact, he introduces the concept of CPI-ME vs. CPI-YOU as a way to illustrate the concept that some individuals are affected differently than others by inflation. [81]

SPIAs produce a constant dollar payout for life. The first SPIA benefit payment received may be worth more than the same benefit payment 30 years down the road. Having said that, the benefit 30 years later serves as a solid dollar income foundation which may not be guaranteed through a systematic withdrawal technique. Assuming 2.3% inflation per year, purchasing power is eroded by half; the SPIA payment in 30 years provides half of the value it used to produce 30 years ago but at least it produces half of it. Running out of funds leaves retirees with nothing.

For the actuarial interested parties out there... Assuming the following:

Assumption:
- Mortality table   2001 CSO Table MNS*
- Interest rate   2%
- Original fund $100,000
- $\ddot{a}_x$ Life annuity, 1 @ age x

*2001 CSO Select and Ultimate Table – Male Nonsmoker – ANB, available on SOA website.

Output:
- $\ddot{a}_{65}$ 14.55
- $\ddot{a}_{75}$ 9.56
- SPIA Benefit at 65 $6,873.68

Scenarios:

A: Buy $100,000 life annuity at age 65, providing $6,873.68 per year.

B: Drawdown $6,873.68 annually on $100,000 portfolio earning 2% per year.

The fair value of the portfolio at age 75 (assuming the individual is still alive and healthy):

A: $65,746 ($6,873.68 * 9.56)

B: $45,129 (Balance at the end of 10 years, starting with $100,000, earning 2% and withdrawing $6,873.68 annually).

Scenario A results in a higher fair value as mortality credit increase the fair value of the portfolio. The flip side to that is that if the person dies within the first 10 years, the fair value of scenario A is zero, as no further payments are due from the life annuity and under scenario B the balance belongs to the heirs.

Going back to inflation, inflation risk increases as retirement time span increases; generally, inflation is of less concern for individuals experiencing a short rather than long retirement. SPIAs typically perform better than fixed income of similar credit quality if the annuity holder lives a long life, as mortality credits boost returns, all else being equal. It is under those circumstances, a long period of time, that inflation has the most potential to hit harder. Higher returns can help cope with inflation.

To cover the potential gap between the inflation adjusted benefit and the actual benefit, a few approaches are available. Additional SPIAs and DIAs starting later is an option that helps increase future total payments, potentially mitigating inflation pressure. Inflation indexed annuities can also be an option. Further, a portion of the remainder of the portfolio invested in traditional invested assets can be invested in inflation adjusted securities such as TIPS or simply in other asset classes such as equities and real estate, which, over the long run, may have a better chance at keeping their value relative to fixed income. As always, diversification is key as future inflation is an unknown and no one knows in advance what any asset class or insurance product will be worth in real terms in the future. Diversification of strategies and product features is always desirable.

Public old-age pension program can also be a great source of inflation protection; for example, in the United States, Social Security provides cost of living protection and can be a good tool to mitigate inflation risk.

Investment Performance and Volatility
Following the AIM approach mitigates the risk of investment volatility. Investment volatility can even be a source of opportunities for savvy investors. Ongoing income may be impacted in times of investment volatility, just as the market value of bequest may be impacted. However, as long as investors are not faced with an obligation to sell securities or funds to provide for living expenses, investment volatility is less of a concern.

Sequence of Returns Risk
Under a systematic withdrawal approach, held assets earn a return each period, yielding to an average return over time. For a given

average return over a long period of time and a constant withdrawal amount, a portfolio will perform much poorly over the long run if returns early on are lower than the average, even if future returns are higher. This is due to the dynamic resulting from selling more assets in a market downturn, leaving less assets in the portfolio for the remainder of the decumulation period. The suggested AIM framework prevents this situation by facilitating sales of assets in opportunistic times only and counting only on the income generated from the assets, as opposed to counting on selling assets in the future during undetermined conditions, hence reducing sequence of return risk.

Liquidity

Liquidity, all else being equal, is a positive feature in an investment. However, liquidity viewed from institutional investors may not be the same as for retirees. Financial institutions often view liquidity as a positive feature in an investment position as the liquid position can be turned into cash fast in order to take advantage of another investment opportunity. Similarly, insurance companies benefit from liquid investments in order to pay claims which can occur randomly. Retirees also need a certain degree of liquidity but for a different purpose; liquidity is typically required to cover unforeseen event. While those liquid assets can be converted to cash quickly, it is important to keep in mind that with those assets gone from the portfolio, the future earning power associated with those assets is also gone.

Pfau explains this well and states that "Liquidity, as it is traditionally defined in securities markets, is of little value as a distinct goal in a long-term retirement income plan." [129]

Further, higher recurring income can reduce the need for liquidity. For example, an unexpected $400 expense for engaging the services of a plumber in the event of a broken pipe may be a liquidity issue for a household earning $2,000 a month and incurring $1,900 monthly expenses. That same plumbing expense may not be a liquidity event for a household earning $10,000 a month and incurring $9,000 monthly expenses. The same holds true in retirement, since the more income a retiree's portfolio of assets and insurance contracts generates, the less need for liquidity, all else being equal.

Lifetime income is generally illiquid in order for the mortality credit mechanism to work properly. Liquidity is important in a portfolio. Liquidity provides flexibility so that retirees can switch asset classes as personal situations change or risk appetite changes. Liquidity can be achieved through holding traditional assets. As always, risks and features need to be considered holistically and hopefully with professional advice. Liquidity is important to cover unexpected obligations including property maintenance or hefty non-recurring health care expenses. However, the totality of a retiree's portfolio does not have to be liquid as those expenses are unexpected and non-recurring. Further, liquidity is expensive in the sense that safe liquid funds such as money market accounts typically provide low attractive returns, all else being equal. The cost of holding liquid assets is high and can translate into reduced ongoing income. It is important to keep an appropriate balance between factors such as liquidity and long-term investment potential.

Fraud

Investment fraud occurs and has the potential of causing significant harm to retirees. Diversification in providers can alleviate this risk. Working with a trusted advisor and/or other professionals also helps alleviate this risk too.

Cognitive Impairment

While some people early in their retirement may have a good grasp of their retirement plan, Alzheimer's, dementia and incapacitation can occur, which can diminish the capacity of retirees to manage money at a time they may be more vulnerable. The AIM provides a clear plan executable by a family member or third party. Using investment income from securities without selling clarifies their role within a portfolio. Further, having a well-documented and executable plan in case of incapacitation is also a good idea.

Credit Downgrade and Default

Credit downgrades and defaults are two risks associated with fixed income investing. Credit downgrade can reduce the value of an investment while default occurs when an obligation is not fulfilled. Ratings play a key role in evaluating this risk. Higher ratings usually translate in a lower probability of default. Higher credit quality is better, all else being equal. However, lower quality issuers exist and may provide the potential for better returns. Retirees need to understand the risk-reward trade-off in order to make a sound decision. Further, diversification among SPIA/DIA contracts and bond holdings also reduces the potential impact of credit default.

Taxation

Taxation, whether in the accumulation or the decumulation phase, is an important consideration. Careful planning and adjustments are important because taxes have a direct impact on a retiree's asset base and ongoing income.

Various DC plans have different tax implications. Understanding the value of the various tax options and how they relate to an individual situation can have a major impact on retirement planning. Tax considerations need to be vetted by the appropriate experts as AIM is executed.

Contrarian Thinking

Increasing Lifetime Income to Leave more Bequest?

How can an individual feeling very bullish on their health with a significant legacy goal and achieve the goal? Having a significant allocation to lifetime income is one hypothetical option. That individual could live on less than the recurrent income and accumulate the difference to leave as a legacy. If he is right, he will have benefitted from higher mortality credits from the lifetime income, therefore increasing returns. However, he runs the risk of getting hit by a bus early in his retirement and failing on his inheritance goals.

Not all income coming from a lifetime income vehicle must be spent, just like a paycheck does not have to be spent in its entirety. Further, a higher allocation to lifetime income can increase bequest for a given spending pattern in the event the retiree lives longer than expected.

Is a SPIA a Very Risky Investment Vehicle?

SPIAs are often seen as a safe financial product that only risk adverse retirees should buy. While SPIAs are typically safe from a credit perspective, an early death can result in a horrible return for the SPIA buyer, potentially less than a major equity downturn.

It is important to see things from various perspectives, rather than entering into financial decisions with preconceived ideas that may not be accurate. Understanding the risk-reward tradeoff from an asset value as well as an income generation perspective can be beneficial.

XVI.   <u>Conclusions</u>

*"Retirement income planning is
one of the most highly personal, complex and
least understood financial journeys
individuals face today."*

— Colin Devine, CFA, CFP, CPA
— Ken Mungan, FSA, MAAA
 2020 [14]

<u>Conclusions</u>

According to the IRI, assets in tax qualified retirement plans in the United States were above $30 trillion at the end of the 3rd quarter of 2019. Further, every day, 10,000 Americans turn 65-year-old. [28] There is an urgent need for individuals to manage their longevity and bequest risks.

A 65-year-old man may die at 65-year-old and one week or may survive until age 110. The financial implications of the two scenarios are completely different for him, his family and society. Individuals must acknowledge the fact that timing of death is unknown. There is a variable cost associated with living. It only makes sense to use some sort of risk pooling mechanism to deal with this risk.

For a hypothetical 65-year-old individual with two children and $5 million worth of invested assets, living on ongoing investment income and expecting to leave the capital of $5 million as a bequest can be a prudent strategy. Depending on market conditions and individual personal situations, selling some assets rationally from time to time during retirement can be a sound approach for spending purposes. The expectation at the beginning of retirement may be to leave $2 million to each child and $1 million to charity at death. If investments perform well, the individual does not live too long and personal situation don't require hefty health or other high spending needs, that bequest may even be higher. Alternatively, if investments perform poorly, the individual lives longer than expected, the individual sold more assets than anticipated and personal situation warrant hefty health care expenses, that bequest may result in $1 million for each child and little left for charity. In other words, the volatility in bequest is present but is not a source of catastrophe because the retiree's wealth can absorb the various shocks. In practice, a minimal segment of the population has amassed this level of wealth (at least at the time this book is written). Repeating the same illustrative exercise with the same individual with one change: he has amassed $1 million at the age of 65 instead of $5 million. This poses a completely different income vs. bequest dilemma. The dollar amount generated by $1 million of capital may be insufficient to live on and selling assets in the future may be necessary. Depending on investment performance, length of retirement and personal situation, bequest may be more than satisfactory but can also be negative as the retiree may run out of funds and rely on his two children to provide for him. Negative bequest is effectively longevity risk. As described through AIM, lifetime income can help calibrate income and bequest expectation combinations and reduce the bequest volatility and avoiding negative bequest.

Like many other facets of life, surveying and utilizing a range of options is often preferable to placing all of one's eggs in a single basket. A reasonable allocation to lifetime income products is worthy of strong consideration.

An approach where various assets and products are purchased over time in small increments to address a retiree's constantly changing needs, risks and environment can provide a stronger basis for retirement. Such a strategy offers the potential to adapt quickly and successfully to both external and internal changes.

As individuals, it is easy to think about short term scenarios such as a drop in the equity market or sudden death but it is much harder to project ourselves in the distant future. This doesn't mean that the far future is unreachable or that we won't live to see it. One out of four 65-year-old male with average health will live beyond age 91, while one out of four 65-year-old female with average health will live beyond age 94. [50] Running out of money at this age is a catastrophe. Imagine reaching an old age, running out of money, forcing you to either depend on your children or societal mechanisms such as Medicaid in the United States. It's a scary thought.

In practice, longevity risk may be a slow bleed and a problem that a retiree can see coming in advance. The problem is that when this occurs, it is most likely too late to react. A more likely scenario is realizing that your resources are not as robust as they might be given your lifespan. In this case, your idea of leaving a sizable bequest may fade away slowly but surely, which may not be a catastrophe. Regardless, without sufficient ongoing income, it's hard to get a handle on spending confidently. Ongoing income from traditional assets and public old-age pension program may not be enough for most to live on. This is why lifetime is so vital. The potential of running out of money will increase over time, becoming more possible just at the point when a retiree feels less comfortable dealing with finances and there's no possibility of going back to work. At that point, there will be little choice: the retiree must cut back on spending, which is problematic given possible threats of inflation, potential health costs and many more possible issues.

Different people may have different approaches at life. Some may feel comfort in knowing that if they die early, their kids will benefit more from their savings and if they die late, their kids won't at all or may even be a financial burden. This gamble isn't necessary. Careful planning avoids this type of roulette. If it's important for an individual to leave a legacy, that individual should plan accordingly. Similarly, if a person has no inheritance motive, it's important to plan accordingly, too, in order to maximize income during retirement.

SPIAs and DIAs are beneficial products in many situations but they are not perfect. They can be expensive as guarantees have explicit and implicit costs associated to them. Just like everything else in life, extremes are usually not desirable. The same goes for income annuities; it is appropriate to strike the right balance between those products and other assets in a portfolio.

Society in general could use more lifetime income to enhance their retirement portfolio [7] [38] [62] [77] without which society may face serious issues. Society, families or friends may face in mass a burden that was not planned for if longevity is not appropriately dealt with from the onset of retirement.

SPIAs and DIAs have a simple design and do not require ongoing contract holder action, which is a win-win situation: Consumers don't have to ask themselves financial questions at a time when it may not be ideal to do so and insurers don't face contract holder behavior risk, which makes the offering more manageable. During working years, individuals face multiple obligations ranging from supporting a family, housing costs, food and utilities to name a few. Further, depending on jurisdictions, health care and education can be quite burdensome too. Lifetime income reverses this dynamic and allows individuals to be in a position where an obligation is owed to them, arguably a good position to be in.

The expression "asset classes" is a widely accepted expression referring to broad groups in which securities and funds of similar characteristics fall. Examples include equities, fixed income and real estate. Conversely, the expression "income classes" is not widely used. Milevsky and Macqueen are one of the very few teams who promote this emphasis of the importance of income during retirement and brought forward the concept of "product allocation". [36] [81] Golden is also in that camp, calling it "Income Allocation Planning". [130] Shemtob addresses this as well through the Retirement Education & Strategy Tool (REST). [123]

AIM differs from traditional systematic withdrawal retirement planning approaches in various ways. Table 13 contrasts the approaches:

Table 13: Traditional Planning vs. AIM

	Systematic Withdrawal	AIM
Longevity risk tradeoff	Income vs. probability of outliving savings	Income vs. bequest
Investment assumptions	Required with risks and tolerances associated with it	Income and bequest estimated and calibrated over time
Expenses vs. income	Expenses determined, assets sold accordingly	Income generated and spent as desired

Experts agree that a portfolio construction and management should be conducted holistically. There is no one single product that possesses the features to protect retirees against every possible risk. The first step in building a holistic, diversified portfolio is considering a retiree's situation from all angles. The second step involves evaluating it from both a balance sheet and an income statement perspective. Applying both steps is the cornerstone of successful retirement planning. After all, it's impossible to know in advance which risk will prevail, from an individual, a societal or an economical perspective. This is why diversification is key. Pre-retirees should assess those balance sheets and income statements and preview their retirement. Looking at the income a portfolio generates a few years before retirement can be a good source of information and even a wake-up call. At that time, pre-retirees have a little more flexibility, can reinvest the income generated from the portfolio, continue to work, delay public old-age pension program benefits and contribute to the asset base. Putting themselves in this mode periodically before retirement, can help make better decisions and get more comfortable with the retirement financial planning dynamic. The need for comprehensive solutions and advice is greater than ever. Thankfully, ventures like Fiduciary Insurance Services, LLC recently emerged specifically to tackle this situation.

Longevity risk represents a major risk for individuals and therefore a great opportunity for financial services firms. It will be interesting to see who will seize this opportunity. Governments also face a threat and it is in everyone's best interest to align solutions and incentives to increase the presence of lifetime income in society in general.

Longevity risk is not simply an isolated risk; it is a risk multiplier. [20] That's because longevity risk increases all the other threats retirees are facing, such as inflation, markets and health care costs.

Retirement planning is, just like many other things in life, a balance between art and science. Methods and approaches are not meant to be prescriptive or one-size fits all. Further, it shouldn't be a "check the box" endeavor; it is more of a dynamic process that can always be adapted to personal situations in the ever-changing world.

The AIM thinking should be applied before retirement; as individuals approach retirement, they can assess their readiness and get a gauge of the types of actions they can take, including working longer or reassessing their asset/income allocation with a financial professional. For example, at age 62, an employed pre-retiree could use the AIM framework as a proxy of what assets and income he faces. If he can work more years, he can do the same exercise at age 63 and compare to what it looked like the prior year. The impact of delaying it public old-age pension program (Social Security in the United States) and an extra year of building assets and therefore future income from employment earnings can give a sense of readiness and desire for retirement, as well as asset/income allocation appropriateness, including lifetime income. As always, those decisions have multiple implications including preferences, market environment and tax strategies to name a few.

On the regulation front, there are encouraging news in the US: the SECURE (Setting Every Community Up for Retirement Enhancement) Act passed in late 2019, offering the potential to encourage the use of lifetime income in retirement planning. Experts generally agree that it is a positive action for the industry. [75] In Quebec, there is progress with what is known as target benefit pension plans, which are effectively DB plans where participants bear some investment and longevity risk. [131]

Corporations, both on the insurance and the asset management side have also shown interest and partnerships to offer more lifetime income solutions to the market.

Building a successful retirement plan is like assembling a winning football team. In order to assemble a winning football team, a coach needs to acquire players with muscle, speed, strength, agility, blocking capabilities and a myriad of other aptitudes. However, each individual player doesn't need to have all these skills. For example, a strong offensive tackle with high blocking capabilities and average speed should not necessarily get discarded based on average speed. This does not mean that speed is not important, but that speed should be a quality perhaps more critical in running backs or wide receivers. The same goes for retirement planning; a myriad of factors and risks should be considered including liquidity, inflation, longevity to name a few but not all products need to possess each of these features. A retirement portfolio needs to be examined holistically, [81] as each product and component of the portfolio brings specific benefits to the overall picture. No one would argue that one needs muscles to win a football game. Assuming Tom Brady can bench-press less than the average NFL football player — which is probably true as the offense and defense tackles most likely boost that average — as a coach, would you put him on the sideline on the premise he does not have enough muscle? The same holds true for SPIAs: they should not be put on the sideline for lack of liquidity, as liquidity can be achieved elsewhere in the portfolio. Further, higher income can potentially decrease the need for liquidity.

Speaking of football players, many professional athletes amass large sums of money early in their lives only to go on and squander their wealth, ending in bankruptcy. Large amounts of money can give a false sense of financial security. The true challenge comes in deciding how to deplete those sums and successfully turn them into ongoing income. Lifetime income is a natural avenue for those athletes because of its ability to turn large assets into an ongoing source of income throughout life, potentially mitigate bankruptcy and dissipation risks.

Taxes are a major consideration and need to be strategized. The best specific approach depends on each individual situation and jurisdiction.

AIM is not an attempt at discrediting other approaches and philosophies. If there was one easy one size fits all approach, retirement planning would be simple. But the many unknowns retirees face, coupled with each individuals' unique stories, makes it impossible to create an auto-pilot solution for everyone. For example, the "Pensionize Your Nest Egg" approach from Milevsky and Macqueen introduces quantitative measures such as the Retirement Sustainability Quotient and other useful metrics to assess a retirement plan. [36] Shemtob also offers a comprehensive approach through REST. [123] Totten and Siegel have also put frameworks together that can help retirees shape their thinking around retirement. [21] Inglis also offers a framework for professionals to work with — A Risk-Based Framework for Making Retirement Income Decisions — that has a focus on income. [69] The Lifetime Income Risk Joint Committee also suggests various approaches to tackle the issue. [132] I encourage the reader to look at other approaches too.

Through this book, many concepts and dilemmas have been brought forward to spark conversations and ideas that can be used in retirement planning. My purpose is to illuminate longevity risk, the tradeoff between bequests and recurring income, the importance of lifetime income and the need for innovation in addressing these situations. By no means am I suggesting that other methods are inappropriate.

Lifetime income helps retirees control how much bequest they will leave and make inheritance less dependent on when they will die. In general terms, for a given spending recurring rate, a higher allocation to lifetime income decreases legacy if the retiree dies earlier than expected and increases inheritance if the retiree lives longer than expected, all else being equal. For a large segment of society, lifetime income offers an individual greater control over their financial future, grants additional security to their family and allows an individual to exert a much greater confidence in spending as well as control of their desired inheritance amount.

The AIM is a tool to assess the key questions in retirement planning and allow a retiree to be in control and achieve their goals. Retirement portfolio construction and management is not a perfect science. As I've mentioned throughout the book, designing a portfolio for flexibility and adaptability makes it easier to achieve big picture goals.

Working with a trusted financial advisor or other financial professional to facilitate holistic retirement planning amid the unique tax, risk and jurisdictional challenges can help build a successful and secure retirement.

Many individuals face longevity risk. Hopefully, society as a whole will react before we can start observing the negative effects, as opposed to waiting until the catastrophe occurs.

Appendices

Basis and Terminology for Illustrative Examples

Internal Rate of Return

The internal rate of return (IRR) consists of the rate of return of an investment. For example, if an investment of $100 is expected pay off $105 in one year, the IRR on the investment is 5%.

Fair Value

The term fair value is used to assess assets, insurance contracts and other benefits on a comparable basis for the illustrative examples. Fair value in this context should not be confused with accounting definitions.

For publicly traded assets, the market value will be used as the fair value. For assets not publicly traded such as private equities and real estate, appraisals or comparable can be used. For assets and benefits that are not necessarily tradable, the price of a comparable asset or benefit will be used. For example, the fair value of a DB Plan can be estimated with the price of a SPIA for a similar benefit at a given age. Health at a given time is also a determining factor in assessing the value of such contract. Art and jewelry can also have a fair value but are typically illiquid and hard to get a reasonable appraisal for; they are often used for legacy purposes.

Ongoing Income

Concept

During working years, people typically count on their salaries, commissions or other forms of compensations to generate recurring income to pay for living expenses, debt, investments or other cash outflows. During retirement, income from assets fills the role of salary. However, people typically will have one, sometimes two, jobs at a particular point in time. Assets operate in a different way because people can own multiple assets at a given point in time and add on or dispose of those in different ways and at different periods of time. Ongoing income in retirement consist of expected recurrent cash flows generated from assets or insurance contracts. While not perfectly comparable, ongoing income during the accumulation phase of retirement is typically a salary; recurring income during the decumulation phase of retirement is typically investment revenues generated from assets (such as dividends from stocks and coupons from bonds) and lifetime income (such as SPIA/DIA benefits or public old-age pension program lifetime benefits). While nothing is guaranteed as employees can be fired, demoted or furloughed and companies have defaulted on bonds or cut dividends, those sources of income are typically reliable and can form a basis for financial planning.

Asset allocation is a quite common practice in retirement planning and the investment community in general. Income allocation has gotten significantly less attention, but some individuals have paid attention to it. For example, Golden discusses the concept of Income Allocation Planning in "From Savings to Income". [133] Milevsky discusses "product allocation". [36] [81] Shemtob also discusses income in the REST Analyser. [123] Another example of the importance of income is illustrated in Cloke's Thrive University, referring to thrive income distribution system. [134] Pfau, Tomlinson and Vernon offer the concept of Retirement Income Generators (RIGs). [31]

Common Assets

This segment will discuss investment revenues generated from various assets commonly owned by individuals.

Bonds

Governments and corporations routinely issue debt to finance their operations, usually in the form of bonds. While there are a wide variety of bond structures, bonds are typically issued on a face amount basis, are scheduled to pay interest periodically and mature at a pre-determined date.

Looking at an illustrative example, a corporation issues a $1,000 bond with 5% coupons maturing in 20 years; the investor pays upfront the face amount of $1,000, expects to receive $50 per year for 20 years and expects to receive his principal back of $1,000 in 20 years. The coupon payment, in this simple illustrative example $50, is the ongoing income the investor can count on.

Income from this asset class is expected to stay steady as a corporation's obligations on debt does not change over time. Coupons and principal may not be paid in the event of bankruptcy.

Equities
Corporations effectively gather resources together with the goal of generating earnings. Corporations are owned by individuals or institutions through shares of equity in the company. Companies issue new equity to finance their operations, usually in the form of common stock. Stocks can be traded in public markets or privately. Earnings generated by companies can either be reinvested in the enterprise or redistributed to the owners of the company, the shareholders.

Looking at an illustrative example, corporation XYZ issues 1,000 shares of common stock $10. Each share currently pays $0.10 dividend. The investor pays upfront the cost of the 1000 shares, so $10,000 and expects to receive $100 per year. The dividend payment, in this example $100, is the ongoing income the investor can count on.

Income from this asset class is typically expected to grow over the long run as a corporation's goal is to maximize shareholder value in the long run. Dividends may also be decreased. Companies can pay a high portion of their earnings in dividends or can reinvest a high portion of their earnings back in the firm. Companies also have other avenues to return capital to shareholders.

Real Estate and Alternative Assets
Real estate properties can be owned directly or through other ownership structures such as funds or partnerships. There are usually three reasons behind direct real estate ownerships: the owner plans on using the property, they plan on renting it out for income or they plan on selling the property. A person's primary residence is typically not rented out and would potentially generate no income (or negative

income including maintenance or taxes). However, there is the potential to make money from renting out a room or a floor of your house through gig economy platforms. Investment properties typically earn rental income.

For example, an individual buys building XYZ for $1 million, expects to collect $100,000 in rental revenues annually and expects to pay expenses of $60,000 in maintenance and administration annually, which would create an annual profit of $40,000. He further expects to retain 25% of the profits within the business and dividend out 75% of the profits and can expect to receive $30,000 per year. The investor pays upfront the cost of the property, so $1 million and expects to receive $30,000 per year. The dividend part of the net income, in this example $30,000, is the ongoing income the investor can count on. The same owner can have the same earning details but choose to retain 75% of the earnings within the business and dividend out 25%. In this case, the dividend would be $10,000 and that would be the ongoing income the investor can count on. With the extra funds kept in the business, the owner could pay for housing improvements, in the hope of generating higher earnings in the future and potentially a higher dividend in the future. These strategies need to be assessed with the appropriate professionals.

Family businesses
Individuals or families may own a business in which a significant portion of their wealth is tied up into the business. Recurring income can be complex as ownership and employment arrangements can differ from traditional structures. Nevertheless, recurring income generated from a family business can be considered as ongoing income.

Contrast
Each of those investments provide different types of protections and risk vs. reward characteristics. For example, some corporations issue both bonds and stocks; coupons from bonds are typically predetermined and not altered. However, stock dividends generally have no obligations associated to them and can increase or decrease. From that perspective, bonds are typically viewed as less risky than stocks. That's because for a given company issuing bonds and stocks, bondholders will be paid before shareholders in case of financial difficulties.

On the other hand, stocks typically provide more upside in income or value than bonds. There is simply a different risk reward tradeoff between the two. Further, stocks paying a high dividend are not necessarily better than the ones who pay lower or no dividends. The dynamic of dividend payment vs. future dividend payment and shareholder value creation for a stock or a fund need to be understood and professional advice is typically warranted.

Lifetime income
Lifetime income is also a form of ongoing income.

SPIAs
A SPIA is a simple insurance contract where the contract holder pays an upfront premium to the insurance company in exchange for recurring guaranteed benefit payments while the contract holder is alive.

For example, a contract holder can buy a SPIA by writing a $10,000 check to an insurance company and that insurance company will pay the contract holder $700 per year for the rest of the person's life. The benefit in this case is $700 of ongoing income an individual can count on.

DIA
A DIA is the same as a SPIA except that the contract holder receives payments later. Those benefits are recurring income an individual can count on, with a caveat that no income will be available for a certain period of time.

Guaranteed Living Benefits on VAs and FIAs
Guaranteed living benefits on VAs and FIAs come in many flavors and can also provide ongoing income one can count on.

Survival Sharing like Structures
A Survival Sharing offers a payout similar to a SPIA except that the mortality and the investment risks are transferred internally to a group of people. Depending on the experience and the performance of the pool, income may increase or decrease but the income received from the participation in the vehicle is ongoing income an individual can count on.

Defined Benefit Pension Plan
It used to be customary for employers to offer DB plans for their employees. This type of plan experienced a significant decline in

popularity across the globe; however, some of these plans still exist and are still active, especially in the public sectors. A DB plan provides guaranteed income in a fashion like a SPIA except that it is offered by an employer and typically depends on length of service, compensation during working years and plan design. Those benefits are recurring income an individual can count on.

Public Old-Age Pension Program

Most countries provide mandatory public old-age pension program offering benefits and have required contributions. In North American, Social Security in the United States and Canada Pension Plan in Canada are good examples of that. Such benefit provides a periodical benefit that is offered for life like a SPIA except that it is offered by the government and it typically depends on working earnings and time the benefit is elected. It may offer inflation protection. Those benefits are ongoing income an individual can count on.

Retiree Himself

Retirees themselves are not an income class but some retirees have the potential to produce income through retirement. Retirees may work or own businesses through retirement, depending on skills, health, ability, need and willingness.

Wrapping up Ongoing Income

Ongoing income consist of reliable income retirees can count on and plan accordingly. It serves as a basis for planning, just like revenues during working years can serve as a basis for planning. Ongoing income from assets and insurance contracts, just like revenues from employment is not necessarily guaranteed. Each asset class and insurance product have their own set of risk reward tradeoff, both from asset value and income generating perspectives. Understanding those tradeoffs in a holistic view over time with a financial professional is key.

The main difference between ongoing income from traditional assets and lifetime income is that assets are meant to be kept and investors can hope to keep the capital with potential appreciation, while capital is meant to be consumed through lifetime income vehicles. Therefore, lifetime income, all else being equal, increases expected ongoing income and reduces expected bequest.

References

1. **Merton, Robert C.** The Crisis in Retirement Planning. *Harvard Business Review.* 2014, July–August 2014.

2. **U.S. Census Bureau.** *An Aging Nation: Projected Number of Children and Older Adults.* s.l. : U.S. Census Bureau, 2018.

3. **LIMRA Secure Retirement Institute.** *The Retirement Income Reference Book - Fourth Edition.* s.l. : LIMRA, 2018.

4. *Americans are Confronted by a Looming Retirement Income Shortfall.* **Alliance for Lifetime Income.** s.l. : Alliance for Lifetime Income, July 31, 2019.

5. **Yaari, Menahem E.** Uncertain Lifetime, Life Insurance and the Theory of the Consumer. *The Review of Economic Studies.* 1965, Vol. 32, 2, pp. 137-150.

6. **McFarland, Brendan.** Retirement Offerings in the Fortune 500: A Retrospective. *Insider.* February 2018, Vol. 28.

7. **Benartzi, Shlomo, Previtero, Alessandro and Thaler, Richard H.** Annuitization Puzzles. *Journal of Economic Perspectives.* 2011, Vol. 25, pp. 143–164.

8. **Pechter, Kerry.** Why Is Income Planning So Hard? *Retirement Income Journal.* July 2, 2020.

9. **Haid, Jennifer A., Chan, Michael and Raham, Christopher G.** *Living to 100: Insights on the Challenges and Opportunities of Longevity: Literature Review: 2002 through 2011.* s.l. : Society of Actuaries, 2013.

10. **Pechter, Kerry.** Seeking 'Ambidextrous Advisers'. *Retirement Income Journal.* January 9, 2020.

11. **Hegna, Tom.** *Retirement Income Masters: Secrets of the Pros.* Boston : Acanthus, 2013. 978-0-9890001-7-8.

12. **Milevsky, Moshe A.** *The 7 Most Important Equations for your Retirement.* Mississauga : Wiley, 2012. 978-1-1182915-3-5.

13. **Warshawsky, Mark J.** *Retirement Income: Risks and Strategies.* Cambridge : MIT Press, 2012. 978-0-262-01693-3.

14. **Devine, Colin and Mungan, Ken.** *Planning for Retirement Income Within an Increasingly Volatile and Uncertain World.* s.l. : Alliance for Lifetime Income, 2020.

15. *La retraite, 25 ans plus tôt.* **Bérubé, Nicolas.** s.l. : La Presse, Octobrer 11, 2020, La Presse.

16. **Milevsky, Moshe A.** *Life Annuities: An Optimal Product for Retirement Income.* Charlottesville, VA : CFA Insitute, 2013. 978-1-934667-56-9.

17. **Markowitz, Harry M.** Individual versus Institutional Investing. *Financial Services Review.* 1991, Vol. 1, 1, pp. 1-8.

18. **Lifetime Income Risk Joint Task Force.** *Risky Business: Living Longer Without Income for Life.* Washington : American Academy of Actuaries, 2013. A Public Policy Discussion Paper.

19. **Lussier, Jacques.** *SECURE RETIREMENT Connecting Financial Theory and Human Behavior.* s.l. : CFA Institute Research Foundation, 2019. MONOGRAPH. 978-1-944960-81-0.

20. **Hegna, Tom.** *Pay Checks and Play Checks.* Boston : Acanthus, 2011. 978-0984217380.

21. **Totten, Thomas L. and Siegel, Laurence B.** Combining Conventional Investing with a Lifetime Income Guarantee: A Blueprint for Retirement Security. *The Journal of Retirement.* 2019, Vol. 6, 4, pp. 45-59.

22. **Pechter, Kerry.** Applying Actuarial Science to Income Planning. *Retirement Income Journal.* January 17, 2020.

23. **Pickett, Erik.** *Top Charts US – Life expectancy doesn't tell the whole story.* s.l. : Club Vita, 2020.

24. **American Academy Of Actuaries.** *Retirement Income Options in Employer-Sponsored Defined Contribution Plans.* Washington : American Academy Of Actuaries, 2017. Position Statement.

25. **Government Accountability Office.** *Retirement Income Ensuring Income Throughout Retirement Requires Difficult Choices.* Washington : Government Accountability Office, 2011.

26. **Gandhi, Amish.** *Investing in (and for) Our Future.* Geneva : World Economic Forum, 2019. White Paper.

27. **International Monetary Fund.** *Global Financial Stability Report.* Washington : International Monetary Fund, 2012. 978-1-61635-247-9.

28. **Insured Retirement Institute.** *State of the Insured Retirement Industry.* Washington : Insured Retirement Institute (IRI), 2020.

29. **D'Amours, Alban.** *Innover pour Pérenniser le Système de Retraite.* Québec : Comité d'experts sur l'avenir du système de retraite québécois, 2013. 978-2-550-67505-1.

30. **Caron, Bruno and Devine, Colin.** Lifetime Income Solutions for DC Plans: Survival Sharing. *Plan Consultant.* 2017, Vol. Spring, 2017, pp. 30-35.

31. **Pfau, Wade, Tomlinson, Joe and Vernon, Steve.** *Viability of the Spend Safely in Retirement Strategy.* s.l. : Stanford Center on Longevity, 2019.

32. **Alliance for Lifetime Income.** Alliance for Lifetime Income. [Online] 2019. https://www.allianceforlifetimeincome.org/#home.

33. **Lifetime Income Risk Joint Committee.** Lifetime Income Risk Joint Committee. *American Academy of Actuaries.* [Online] https://www.actuary.org/committees/dynamic/LITF.

34. *Lifetime Income: Risks and Solutions.* **Abkemeier, Noel, et al.** s.l. : American Academy of Actuaries, 2012.

35. **Golden, Jerry.** Are Income Annuities Fair? *Kiplinger.* March 19, 2019.

36. **Milevsky, Moshe A. and Macqueen, Alexandra.** *Pensionize your Nest Egg.* Hoboken : Wiley, 2015. 9781119025252.

37. **Caron, Bruno and Devine, Colin.** Bequest goals: more than just an issue for the wealthy. *Think Advisor.* August 9, 2016.

38. **Dellinger, Jeffrey K.** *The Handbook of Variable Income Annuities.* Hoboken : John Wiley & Sons, 2006. 13-978-0-471-73382-9.

39. **Golden, Jerry.** Don't Bet your Retirement on Monte Carlo Models. *Kiplinger.* November 14, 2019.

40. **Finke, Michael and Pfau, Wade.** *It's More than Money.* Des Moines : Principal, 2019.

41. **Vernon, Steve.** The Magic Formula for Retirement Security. *Moneywatch.* NOVEMBER 27, 2012.

42. **Cooper, Cheryl R. and Li, Zhe.** *Saving for Retirement: Household Decisionmaking and Policy Options.* s.l. : Congressional Research Service, 2020.

43. *Concurrent Session 5B: What Is Different Today for Post-retirement Financial Planning?* **Burden, Tamara.** Orlando, Fl. : Society of Actuaries, 2017. Living to 100 Symposium.

44. **DiCenzo, Jodi.** *Employees' Retirement Choices, Perceptions and Understanding: A Review of Selected Survey and Empirical Behavioral Decision-Making Research.* s.l. : Society of Actuaries, 2014.

45. **Ferrante-Schepis, Maria and Maddock, G. Michael.** *Flirting With The Uninterested.* Charleston : Advantage, 2012. 978-159932-369-5.

46. **Brown, Robert and Gottlieb, Leon.** *Introduction to Ratemaking and Loss Reserving for Property and Casualty Insurance.* Winsted : Actex, 2001.

47. **Pfau, Wade.** Deciphering the Annuity Puzzle: Practical Guidance for Advisors. *Advisor Perspectives.* July 24, 2012.

48. **Dellinger, Jeffrey K.** *When to Commence Income Annuities.* s.l. : Society of Actuaries, 2011. Monograph.

49. **Social Security.** Period Life Tables. [Online] 2019. https://www.ssa.gov/oact/HistEst/PerLifeTables/2019/PerLifeTable s2019.html.

50. **American Academy of Actuaries and Society of Actuaries.** Actuaries Longevity Illustrator. *Actuaries Longevity Illustrator.* [Online] American Academy of Actuaries and Society of Actuaries. [Cited: September 3, 2020.] http://www.longevityillustrator.org/.

51. **O'Flinn, Chris and Schirripa, Felix.** *Revisiting Retirement Withdrawal Plans and their Historical Rates of Return.* s.l. : O'Flinn Schirripa, 2010. Monographs.

52. **Mathew Greenwald Associates, Inc.; Employee Benefit Research Institute.** *2011 Risks and Process of Retirement Survey Report of Findings.* hh. s.l. : Society of Actuaries, 2012.

53. *U.S. Health Care Spending Highest Among Developed Countries.* **Johns Hopkins Bloomberg School of Public Health.** Baltimore, MD : s.n., January 7, 2019.

54. **Rosen, Sally, Maehr, Bridget and Zazzera, Joseph.** *2020 Review & Preview: US Health.* Oldwick, NJ : AM Best, 2020. Best's Market Segment Report.

55. **Forman, Jonathan B.** Removing the Legal Impediments to Offering Lifetime Annuities in Pension Plans. *Connecticut Insurance Law Journal.* 2016, Vol. 23, 1, pp. 31-141.

56. **Blanchett, David M. and Finke, Michael.** Should Annuities Be Purchased with Tax-Sheltered Assets? *Journal of Financial Services Professionals.* August 2, 2019, Vol. 73, 3.

57. **Forman, Jonathan B.** *Workers and Retirees Could Pool Risk Wit Tontine Annuities, Tontine Pensions and Survivor Funds.* s.l. : Society of Actuaries, 2018. Essay.

58. **MacDonald, Bonnie-Jeanne, et al.** Research and Reality - A Literature Review on Drawing Down Retirement Financial Savings. *North American Actuarial Journal.* September 11, 2013, Vol. 17, 3, pp. 181-215.

59. *When Others Die, Tontine Investors Win.* **Verde, Tom.** s.l. : The New York Times, March 24, 2017, The New York Times.

60. **Milevsky, Moshe A.** Optimal Asset Allocation Towards The End of the Life Cycle: To Annuitize or Not to Annuitize? *The Journal of Risk and Insurance.* 1998, Vol. 65, 3, pp. 401-426.

61. **Horneff, Vanya, Maurer, Raimond and Mitchell, Olivia S.** *Automatic enrollment in 401(k) annuities: Boosting retiree lifetime income.* s.l. : The Brookings Institution, 2019.

62. **Brown, Jeffrey R.** *Life Annuities and Uncertain Lifetimes.* Cambridge : National Bureau of Economic Research, 2004. Research Summary.

63. **Bell, Allison.** Alicia Munnell's Social Security Bridge v. Annuities Income Planning Smackdown. *ThinkAdvisor.* January 3, 2020.

64. **Bowers, Newton L., et al.** *Actuarial Mathematics.* Schaumburg : Society of Actuaries, 1997. 0-938959-46-8.

65. **Vernon, Steve.** *Retirement Game-Changers: Strategies for a Healthy, Financially Secure, and Fulfilling Long Life.* s.l. : Rest-of-Life Communications, 2018. 978-0-9853846-4-7.

66. —. Boost Your Risk-Protected Retirement Income With A Social Security Bridge Payment. *Forbes.* May 26, 2020.

67. **Rappaport, Anna, et al.** Interesting Perspectives on Lifetime Income. *Pension Section News.* January 2013, 82, pp. 19-23.

68. **Pfau, Wade.** *Safety-First Retirement Planning: An Integrated Approach for a Worry-Free Retirement.* Vienna : Retirement Researcher Media, 2019. 978-1945640063.

69. **Inglis, R. Evan.** *A Risk-Based Framework for Making Retirement Income Decisions.* s.l. : Society of Actuaries, 2020. Essay.

70. **Mettler, Gary S.** *Always Keep Your Hands Up.* North Charleston : CreateSpace, 2014. 1499304927.

71. **Milevsky, Moshe A.** *Your Money Milestones.* Upper Saddle River : FT Press, 2010. 0-13-702910-1.

72. **Pechter, Kerry.** 'Safety First' Income Plans, Per Wade Pfau. *Retirement Income Journal.* October 10, 2019.

73. **Kadlec, Dan.** Lifetime Income Stream Key to Retirement Happiness. *Time magazine.* July 30, 2012.

74. **Pechter, Kerry.** *Annuities For Dummies.* Indianapolis : John Wiley & Sons, Inc, 2008. 978-0-470-17889-8.

75. **Richter, Michelle.** *Reframing Retirement Advice Objectives from Asset Management to Income Management: a case for Fiduciary Annuities.* s.l. : Linked In, 2020. Post.

76. **Lexico.** Lexico. *Lexico.* [Online] Oxford, 2020. https://www.lexico.com/en/definition/annuity.

77. **Greenwald & Associates and CANNEX.** *The Top 10 Key Findings A Study Summary of the Sixth Annual Guaranteed Lifetime Income Study (GLIS).* s.l. : Greenwald & Associates and CANNEX, 2020.

78. **Pechter, Kerry.** Annuities Need More Positive 'Positioning'. *Retirement Income Journal.* June 13, 2019.

79. **Pfau, Wade.** Payout Rates and Returns on Income Annuities. *Forbes.* August 27, 2015.

80. **Wikipedia.** Decimation (Roman army). *Wikipedia.* [Online] 2020. https://en.wikipedia.org/wiki/Decimation_(Roman_army).

81. **Milevsky, Moshe A.** *Are you a Stock or a Bond? Create your Own Pension Plan for a Secure Financial Future.* Upper Saddle River : FT Press, 2009. 0-13-712737-5.

82. **Routledge, Richard.** Law of Large Numbers. *Encyclopedia Britannica.* [Online] Encyclopedia Britannica. https://www.britannica.com/science/law-of-large-numbers.

83. **Pechter, Kerry.** Making Income Rise as Health Declines. *Retirement Income Journal.* October 3, 2019.

84. **Iwry, Mark, et al.** *Retirement Tontines: Using a Classical Finance Mechanism as an Alternative Source of Retirement Income.* Washington, DC : Brookings Institution, 2020.

85. **Pechter, Kerry.** She's Got Advice for Life Insurers. *Retirement Income Journal.* October 1, 2020.

86. **Sabin, Michael J.** *Fair Tontine Annuity.* Sunnydale, CA : s.n., 2010. Working Paper.

87. *Payout and Income Annuities.* **Abels, Stephen J. and Leboeuf, Michael J.** New Orleans : Society of Actuaries, 2005. Life Spring Meeting. Vol. 31.

88. *For your retirement planning, count on living until age 95.* **Powell, Robert.** s.l. : USA TODAY, October 5, 2016, USA TODAY.

89. **Lifetime Income Risk Joint Task Force.** *Retiree Lifetime Income: Product Comparisons.* Washington, DC : American Academy of Actuaries, 2015. Issue Brief.

90. **Ritholtz, Barry.** Tackling 'Nastiest, Hardest Problem in Finance'. *Think Advisor.* June 6, 2017.

91. *Meet the People Trying to Put a Friendlier Face on Annuities.* **Lieber, Ron.** s.l. : The New York Times, December 21, 2018, The New York Times.

92. **McClelland, Dean.** *MoneyTalk.Be: Tontines: a solution to the pension crisis and the rebuilding of the economy? No time to lose.* s.l. : LinkedIn, 2020. Post.

93. **Fullmer, Richard K. and Sabin, Michael J.** Individual Tontine Accounts – Yes, Seriously! *Retirement Income Journal.* October 11, 2018.

94. **Fullmer, Richard K.** *Tontines: A Practitioner's Guide to Mortality-Pooled Investments.* s.l. : CFA Institute Research Foundation, 2019. Brief. 978-1-944960-75-9.

95. *Facing up to longevity with old actuarial methods: a comparison of pooled funds and income tontines.* **Bräutigam, Marcel, Guillen, Montserrat and Nielsen, Jens P.** 3, s.l. : The Geneva Papers on Risk and Insurance - Issues and Practice, 2017, Vol. 42, pp. 406-422.

96. **Tuck, Natalie.** *Back to the future.* s.l. : European Pensions, 2020.

97. **McKeever, Kent.** A Short History of Tontines. *Fordham Journal of Corporate & Financial Law.* 2009, Vol. 15, 2, pp. 491-521.

98. **Ransom, Roger L. and Sutch, Richard.** Tontine insurance and the Armstrong investigation: a case of stifled innovation in the american life insurance industry, 1868-1905. *The Journal of Economic History.* 1987, Vol. 47, 2, pp. 379-390.

99. *Japan's Aging Population Breathes New Life Into a Centuries-Old Investment Idea.* **Hayashi, Yuka.** s.l. : The Wall Street Journal, February 25, 2020, The Wall Street Journal.

100. **Chevreau, Jonathan.** Retired Money: How the financial industry may use ALDAs and VLPAs as Longevity Insurance. *Financial Independence Hub.* May 22, 2019.

101. **Milevsky, Moshe A.** Tontines in the Townships of South Africa. *Retirement Income Journal.* September 14, 2017.

102. **Forman, Jonathan B. and Fullmer, Richard K.** Tontine Savings Accounts. *Retirement Income Journal.* June 30, 2020.

103. **Milevsky, Moshe A., et al.** *Annuities Versus Tontines in the 21st Century.* s.l. : Society of Actuaries, 2018.

104. **Milevsky, Moshe A. and Salisbury, Thomas S.** Optimal retirement income tontines. *Insurance: Mathematics and Economics*. September 2015, Vol. 64, pp. 91-105.

105. *Optimal retirement tontines for the 21st century: with reference to mortality derivatives in 1693.* **Milevsky, Moshe A. and Salisbury, Thomas S.** Orlando, FL : Society of Actuaries, 2013. Living to 100 Symposium.

106. **Milevsky, Moshe A.** *King William's Tontine: Why the Retirement Annuity of the Future Should Resemble its Past.* New York : Cambridge University Press, 2015. 978-1-107-07612-9.

107. **Milevsky, Moshe A. and Salisbury, Thomas S.** Equitable Retirement Income Tontines: Mixing Cohorts without Discriminating. September 2016, Vol. 46, 3, pp. 571-604.

108. **Wadsworth, Mike, Findlater, Alec and Boardman, Tom.** *Reinventing Annuities.* s.l. : Staple Inn Actuarial Society, 2001.

109. *The Simple Analytics of a Pooled Annuity Fund.* **Piggott, John, Valdez, Emiliano A. and Detzel, Bettina.** 3, s.l. : American Risk and Insurance Association, September 2005, The Journal of Risk and Insurance, Vol. 72, pp. 497-520.

110. **Stamos, Michael Z.** *Optimal Consumption and Portfolio Choice for Pooled Annuity Funds.* 2007. White Paper.

111. **Sherris, Michael and Qiao, Chao.** Managing Systematic Mortality Risk with Group Self Pooling and Annuitisation Schemes. December 2013, Vol. 80, 4, pp. 949-974.

112. *A Mutual Fund to Yield Annuity-Like Benefits.* **Goldsticker, Ralph P.** 1, s.l. : CFA Institute, January 1, 2007, Financial Analysts Journal, Vol. 63. 0015-198X.

113. **Baker, Tom and Siegelman, Peter.** Tontines for the Invincibles: Enticing Low Risks Into the Health Insurance Pool With an Idea From Insurance History and Behavioral Economics. 2010.

114. **Rotemberg, Julio J.** *Can a Continuously-Liquidating Tontine (or Mutual Inheritance Fund).* s.l. : Harvard Business School, 2009. Working Paper.

115. **Sabin, Michael J.** Fair Tontine Project Page. *Fair Tontine Project Page.* [Online] http://sagedrive.com/fta/index.htm.

116. **Forman, Jonathan B. and Sabin, Michael J.** Tontine Pensions. *Penn Law Review.* 2015, Vol. 163, 3, pp. 755-831.

117. **Fullmer, Richard K. and Sabin, Michael J.** Individual Tontine Accounts. *Journal of Accounting and Finance.* 2019, Vol. 19, 8.

118. *Want Financial Security? Look to the Renaissance.* **Milevsky, Moshe A.** s.l. : The Wall Street Journal, April 21, 2013, The Wall Street Journal.

119. **Caron, Bruno.** *Funding and Distribution of Income Stream Payments for a Period Associated with the Longevity of Participant Individuals. US20140229402 A1* August 14, 2014.

120. **Donnelly, Catherine, Guillén, Montserrat and Nielsen, Jens Perch.** Exchanging uncertain mortality for a cost. *Insurance: Mathematics and Economics.* January 2013, Vol. 52, 1, pp. 65-76.

121. **Seawright, Bob.** The Annuity Puzzle. *Think Advisor.* February 1, 2012.

122. **Golden, Jerry.** How to Boost Retirement Income by Making It Safer. *Kiplinger.* October 4, 2018.

123. **Shemtob, Mark.** Retirement Education & Strategy Tool. *REST.* [Online] 2020. http://www.malbecmania.com/.

124. **Wasserstein, Ron.** George Box: a model statistician. *Significance.* July 8, 2010, Vol. 7, 3, pp. 134-135.

125. **Buffett, Warren.** *Letter to shareholders, 1988.* 1989.

126. **Lifetime Income Risk Joint Task Force.** *Risky business: living longer without income for life actuarial considerations for financial advisers.* s.l. : American Academy of Actuaries, 2015.

127. **Caron, Bruno, Hansen, George and Hopper, Jason.** Long-Term Care Rate Increases Drive Premium, Loss Ratio Remains Volatile. *Best's Special Report.* February 16, 2018.

128. **Fidelity.** *How to plan for rising health care costs.* s.l. : FIDELITY VIEWPOINTS, 2020.

129. **Pfau, Wade.** *How much can I spend in retirement.* McLean : Retirement Researcher Media, 2017. 978-1-945640-02-5.

130. **Golden, Jerry.** Retirement Planning Reinvented. April 2, 2019.

131. **Cabinet du ministre des Finances.** *The Minister of Finance tables Bill 68 to allow the establishment of target benefit pension plans.* October 7, 2020.

132. **Lifetime Income Risk Joint Committee.** *Actuarial Perspectives on Determining a Retirement Income Budget.* Washington, DC : American Academy of Actuaries, 2020. Issue Brief.

133. **Golden, Jerry.** From Savings to Income.

134. **Cloke, Curtis.** Retirement Income Solutions. [Online] https://curtiscloke.com/thrive-university.html.

Acronyms

- $\ddot{a}_x$:   Value of 1 paying for life stating at age x
- AAA: American Academy of Actuaries
- ASPPA: American Society of Pension Professionals and Actuaries
- AIM: Asset to Income Method
- CD: Certificate of Deposit
- CPI: Consumer Price Index
- DB plan: Defined Benefit Pension Plan
- DC plan: Defined Contribution Pension Plan
- DIA: Deferred Income Annuity
- FDA: Fixed Deferred Annuity
- FIA: Fixed Indexed Annuity
- IRI: Insured Retirement Institute
- IRR: Internal Rate of Return
- LTC: Long-Term Care
- QLAC: Qualified Longevity Annuity Contracts
- REST: Retirement Education & Strategy Tool
- RMD: Required Minimum Distribution
- SOA: Society of Actuaries
- SPIA: Single Premium Immediate Annuity
- TSA: Tontine Savings Account
- VA: Variable Annuity
- VIA: Variable Income Annuity

Lists of Tables and Figures

List of Tables

List of Figures

<u>Acknowledgments</u>

This book is the result of many years of engagement with lifetime income, starting with the venture, Survival Sharing, which I started with the help from John Clinton, CPCU, CPA, Colin Devine, CFA, CFP, CPA, Marc Duquette, Efrem Epstein and Michael Pettit.

The American Academy of Actuaries (AAA) Lifetime Income Risk Joint Committee co-led by Noel Abkemeier, FSA, MAAA and Mark Shemtob, FSA, MAAA, EA, MSPA, FCA was also a strong foundation for strengthening my passion on the topic. The group continues to sparkle many interesting and productive conversations after many years, resulting in a vast high-quality body of research and policy recommendations on lifetime income and other retirement issues.

I owe a special thank you to Hélène L'Heureux, dga, FGDC, for offering the professional visual feedback as well as designing the book cover.

As for the architecture of the book, I was fortunate to benefit from strong professional support and I would like to thank Amy E. Buttell for shaping this book in a professional way, much beyond editing. Thanks to David Bernardy for his proofreading expertise.

I owe a special thanks to Colin Devine, CFA, CFP, CPA for the direct involvement in the book, including writing the foreword, the comments and the deep thinking about the concepts advanced in the book. Thank you also for the many years of partnership and mentorship through the various roles and projects we worked on together. I look forward to many more!

I also owe a special thanks to Noel Abkemeier, FSA, MAAA for getting me involved in the first place with the AAA Lifetime Income Risk Joint Committee as well as the leadership and dedication within this space. Further, Noel's contribution to this book was vital; the wisdom, balanced view and the ability to see the multiple dimensions on the topic can be felt through the book. Your broad vision and specialized expertise were most certainly appreciated!

I would also like to thank Mark Shemtob, FSA, MAAA, EA, MSPA, FCA for his challenging questions, stimulating discussions through the years and direct comments on the content of the book. I strongly benefited from your unique perspective; your ability to combine deep thinking and practical knowledge was felt throughout the book.

I would also like to thank the following professionals and experts who offered direct constructive feedback and insights on the book: Francis Baillargeon, Pierre Caron, Yanick Chainey, FSA, FCIA, Alexandre Gagnon, Jérôme Grenier, Richard Fullmer, CFA, Moshe A. Milevsky, PhD, Michelle Richter, MBA, Cornelia Spiegel.

I would also like to thank my AM Best inner circle — Kenneth A. Frino, George Hansen, FSA, MAAA, Ken Johnson, CFA, CAIA, FRM, Edward Kohlberg, CLU, Anthony McSwieney, Rosemarie Mirabella, CPA, CFA, William Pargeans, Michael Porcelli, FSA, Thomas Rosendale, FLMI, CLU, ChFC and Louis Silvers, ASA, MAAA, CERA — for the elevating my knowledge, sharing their savoir faire, strengthening my expertise and sharpening my critical thinking in the areas of insurance and investments. I would also like to thank my other colleagues — Michael Adams, CLU, Igor Bass, Keith Behrmann, CFA, CAIA, ChFC, CLU, Adrienne Carchia, Matthew Dachowski, James Gillard, Yaroslav Hlum, FSA, MAAA, Stefan Holzberger, CPA, Jason Hopper, Stephen A. Irwin, Jia Jian, CFA, FRM, FLMI, Wayne Kaminsky, Chris Lewis, Sean Lynch, Sridhar Manyem, David Marek, Mary Marzano, Maura McGuigan, Erik Miller, CFA, Anastasios Mironidis, Matthew Mosher, FCAS, MAAA, CERA, Thomas Mount, ACAS, MAAA, CERA, Shauna Nelson, Bill Payton, James Peavy, Christopher Sharkey, Al Slavin, Kate Steffanelli, FLMI, Kevin Varvaro and Frank Walko — as well as the AM Best Global Reinsurance, Insurance Linked Securities, Health, P&C and Composite Analytical Groups for the collaborative efforts in the field through the years and also for making me smarter on the broad topics of insurance and investments.

I would also like to thank the experts, researchers, bloggers, influencers, authors, scholars and entrepreneurs in the retirement income space for their work in the space and most specifically the ones with whom I've kept an open dialogue over the years, including Noel Abkemeier, FSA, MAAA, Yanick Chainey, FSA, FCIA, Colin Devine, CFA, CFP, CPA, Maria Ferrante-Schepis, Richard Fullmer, CFA, Alexandre Gagnon, FSA, EA, CFA, Tom Hegna, CLU, ChFC, CASL, Jerry Golden, MAAA, Michael Gordon, Benoit Labrosse, FSA, MAAA, CERA, Charles-Antoine Laplante, FSA, MAAA, ACIA, Dean McClelland, Moshe A. Milevsky, PhD, Gary Mettler, CFP, CEBS, Kerry Pechter, Wade Pfau, PhD, CFA, RICP, Michelle Richter, MBA, Mark Shemtob, FSA, MAAA, EA, MSPA, FCA, Prakash Shimpi, FSA, MAAA, CERA, Ramsey Smith, Cornelia Spiegel, Paul Tyler and Steve Vernon, FSA.

I would like to thank the various efforts, spearheaded by my Mélanie St-Amour, related to all facets related to bringing this book forward. We benefited from expertise from many specialists who have shared their knowledge and experience in various areas: Alexandre Archambault, Amy E. Buttell, Ann Champoux, Marc Duquette, Nicole Handy, Ian Hinchcliffe, Dochtor Kennedy, Françoise L'Heureux, Hélène L'Heureux, dga, FGDC, Carolyne Léger and Kerry Pechter.

I feel fortunate to be surrounded by a wonderful family and group of friends, including some with various expertise and great vision who have generously took the time to provide thoughtful feedback on the book, including Alexandre Archambault, Pierre Caron, Yanick Chainey, FSA, FCIA, Ann Champoux, Marc Duquette, Alexandre Gagnon, FSA, EA, CFA, Jérôme Grenier, Nicole Handy, Benoit Labrosse, FSA, MAAA, CERA, Charles-Antoine Laplante, FSA, MAAA, ACIA, Françoise L'Heureux, Hélène L'Heureux, dga, FGDC, Carolyne Léger, Carl Lussier, FCAS and Michael Pettit. My close friend Francis Baillargeon who never missed an opportunity to be there for me over the many decades also shared his valuable wisdom, intelligence and expertise on the book; Merci encore une fois!

I would like to thank my parents Marthe and Michel for their continued support, inspiration and love. Last but not least, I would like to thank my wife Mélanie for your love, determination and dedication to our family. With your parents, Louise and Normand, all five contributed directly to this book by taking good care of our two loves, Annabelle and Elliott, while I was writing this book... Merci à vous tous!

Index

M

About Colin Devine

Colin Devine is an Operating Partner with Health Catalyst Capital, a venture capital fund that in high-growth InsurTech-enabled businesses. He is also a Research Fellow for the Alliance for Lifetime Income, a nonprofit 501(c)(6) organization focused on helping educate Americans on the risk of outliving their savings so they can enjoy their retirement. A recognized industry thought leader, Colin is a frequent guest speaker at conferences and corporate events.

During his 15-year tenure with Smith Barney/Citigroup he was consistently ranked among the top sell-side equity analysts in the insurance sector. Colin was on the Institutional Investor All-America Research Team for 14 straight years including 10 consecutive years where he held the #1/#2 ranking in the Life Insurance Equity Research category. Smart Money Magazine named him one of the "Last Honest Analysts"

Colin also held various roles, including Managing Director at Jefferies, a Director in Standard & Poor's Insurance Ratings group and a Vice-President of a major Canadian life insurer where he was involved in investment, risk management, treasury and corporate development initiatives. He began his career with a large Canadian commercial bank.

His involvement in the broad retirement income space has been discussed in various general media outlets, including Barron's, Jim Cramer, the New York Times and the Wall Street Journal. He has also published articles in specialized and professional organizations, including AM Best, ASPPA, the SOA and ThinkAdvisor.

Colin is a Chartered Financial Analyst (CFA), Chartered Professional Accountant (CPA) and a Certified Financial Planner (CFP). He holds an MBA in Finance from the Schulich School of Business at York University in Toronto and a Bachelor of Science in Biology from the University of Guelph.

He currently lives in New York City, NY, USA.

About the Author

Bruno Caron is a Senior Financial Analyst at AM Best. He is an actuary with experiences across various sectors of the financial services industry in North America: consulting, life insurance company, start-up company, sell-side equity research and credit ratings.

Through this book, he offers a unique perspective, combining investment and insurance expertise. Over the past years, he has challenged the norms. His entrepreneurial nature and appetite for innovation drove the efforts behind this book. He has deep life insurance industry experience as well as extensive company knowledge, a solid equity market background, familiarity with rating dynamics and a passion for longevity risk.

Before AM Best, he held prior roles as an Equity Research Associate at Jefferies and CEO and Founder of Survival Sharing. He also held roles at New York Life and Willis Towers Watson.

His involvement in the broad insurance space has been discussed in various general media outlets, including Barron's, the New York Times and Reuters. He has also published articles in specialized and professional organizations, including the AAA, AM Best, ASPPA, the SOA and ThinkAdvisor.

He is the ASPPA 2016 Ed Burrows Award recipient and a nominee for the inaugural 2019 Insurance Careers Movement Emerging Leaders Conference.

Bruno is a Fellow of the Society of Actuaries (FSA) and a Member of the American Academy of Actuaries (MAAA). He is also a member of the AAA Lifetime Income Risk Joint Committee. He holds an Honors Bachelor in Mathematics from the University of Waterloo, majoring in Actuarial Sciences and Statistics.

He currently lives in Maplewood, NJ, USA with his wife and their two children.

Made in the USA
Middletown, DE
20 January 2021

Bruno Caron is a Senior Financial Analyst at AM Best.
He is an actuary with experiences across various sectors of
the financial services industry in North America: consulting,
life insurance company, start-up company, sell-side equity
research and credit ratings.

Through this book, he offers a unique perspective, combining
investment and insurance expertise. Over the past years,
he has challenged the norms. His entrepreneurial nature
and appetite for innovation drove the efforts behind this
book. He has deep life insurance industry experience as
well as extensive company knowledge, a solid equity market
background, familiarity with rating dynamics and a passion
for longevity risk.

Before AM Best, he held prior roles as an Equity Research
Associate at Jefferies and CEO and Founder of Survival
Sharing. He also held roles at New York Life and
Willis Towers Watson.

His involvement in the broad insurance space has been
discussed in various general media outlets, including
Barron's, the New York Times and Reuters. He has
also published articles in specialized and professional
organizations, including the AAA, AM Best, ASPPA, the SOA
and ThinkAdvisor.

He is the ASPPA 2016 Ed Burrows Award recipient and
a nominee for the inaugural 2019 Insurance Careers
Movement Emerging Leaders Conference.

Bruno is a Fellow of the Society of Actuaries (FSA) and a
Member of the American Academy of Actuaries (MAAA).
He is also a member of the AAA Lifetime Income Risk Joint
Committee. He holds an Honors Bachelor in Mathematics
from the University of Waterloo, majoring in Actuarial
Sciences and Statistics.

He currently lives in Maplewood, NJ, USA with his wife
and their two children.

ISBN 9781082296246

9000

9 781082 296246